Twisters
in the
Heartland

Twisters in the Heartland

By

TIM D. MOSIER

RIVERCROSS PUBLISHING, INC
New York ● Orlando

Copyright © 1998 by Tim D. Mosier

ISBN: 1-58141-002-6

Library of Congress Catalog Card Number: 98-24664

Second printing

Library of Congress Cataloging-in-Publication Data

Mosier, Tim D., 1952–
    Twisters in the heartland / by Tim D. Mosier.
      p.   cm.
    ISBN 1-58141-002-6
    1. Tornadoes—Middle West—Popular works. 2. Tornadoes—Southern States—Popular works. 3. Severe storms—Middle West—Popular works. 4. Meteorological services—United States—Popular works.
I. Title.
QC955.5.U6M35 1998
551.55'3'0978—dc21
                                        98-24664
                                           CIP

This book is dedicated to the courageous volunteers of the Sedalia-Pettis County Emergency Management Agency, to my departed friend, John Burford, and to our Father in heaven, who rides with me on every chase.

Acknowledgments

I would like to express my most sincere appreciation to the following. Without their support this book could not have been published.

Central Missouri News
Mary McClaughlin
Missouri Emergency Preparedness Agency
Missouri Army National Guard
My family and friends who gave me much-needed support
Sedalia, Missouri Police Department
Sedalia Democrat Newspaper
Sedalia-Pettis County Missouri Emergency Management Agency
The Eliot Stein Show
The National Weather Service
Vision Computer Technology

Contents

Preface

Twisters in the Heartland is an intriguing and informative book that describes actual tornado events from the author's first hand perspective as a tornado spotter. The genesis, development, cause of certain tornadoes and their threats to human life and property are described in layman's terms, making the book easy to understand and exciting to read.

Thousands of Americans have lost their lives to tornados. We can not prevent them from occurring, but we can reduce the number of lives lost to killer tornados through public education and by increasing lifesaving warning time.

Twisters in the Heartland describes sheltering plans and procedures which you can use to better your chances of surviving a tornado. The book also describes the partnership between severe weather spotters and National Weather Service meteorologists, as they work together to provide timely warning for communities all over this country.

Though I believe tornados should not be a phenomenon which should be feared I do believe they should be respected. Each year many Americans are killed by tornados, many of these deaths can be prevented or drastically reduced by following simple safety rules and by pre-planning sheltering needs.

I ask each reader to take the necessary time to make family and/or work place sheltering plans for a tornado event well before the need arises. The steps you take before a tornado strikes is crucial to survival. I hope you enjoy reading *Twisters in the Heartland* as much as I have enjoyed writing the book.

Tim D. Mosier

Twisters
in the
Heartland

Chapter One

Understanding Tornados and Basic Severe Weather Safety Concepts

Man has marveled at the untamed power of natural phenomenona since the beginning of time. It is no wonder we continue to do so today. Earthquakes, tidal waves, volcanos, hurricanes, floods; the list goes on and on. However, one natural phenomenon in particular stands out among the rest. The awesome and powerful tornado. Concentrating all of its power into one localized area of destruction the tornado has no rival. No other natural occurrence can equal its strength or relentless devastation. It strikes anywhere, anytime and with little or no warning. Even our modern architectural accomplishments are no match for this fearsome predator.

Tornadoes kill and injure scores of Americans each year leaving behind a staggering toll of death, injury and damage totaling millions of dollars. Over the last fifty years scientists and meteorologists have gained a wealth of knowledge and data concerning the birth, life, and death of tornados. Much of this data comes from specially trained tornado hunters, or tornado chasers who provide the National Weather Service critical, up close information which is analyzed by meteorologists all over the world. The Severe Storms Laboratory in Norman, Oklahoma is a natural headquarters for this project as many tornado events occur in the area each year. But even with all our scientific instruments and know—how there is still a great deal we do not know.

Tornados have plagued mankind in the past and will most certainly continue to do so in the future. Since we can not prevent tornados from occurring we must take advantage of the information we have and use it to our own advantage. Pre-planning our tornado sheltering needs will go a long way toward reducing the loss of life and injury. Since there is no doubt tornados will strike our communities in the future, the proposition is a simple one: either we prepare for their arrival and survive or ignore what we have learned and become a statistic.

Our personal attitudes and views concerning severe weather and tornado preparedness are as varied and diverse as the people who live in our country. For example, I have taught hundreds of severe weather awareness programs over the years. Most of those who attend want to know how to prepare their homes and businesses for a tornadic event; others attend because their employers or supervisors made their attendance mandatory. It is unfortunate we still have those few who refuse to help themselves and their families. People with this kind of mentality are the very ones who most likely will become statistics. While I do not condone their attitude I do understand it. Some people falsely believe that because their homes and families are with them today they will surely be there tomorrow. After all, they have lived this long without planning for their safety, right? Definitely not. This reasoning is not only dangerous, it can be fatal.

Severe weather awareness is not a subject which is or hard to remember. True we are bombarded with enough information each day to confuse any computer on the market today; however, tornados pose a threat to our very existence which makes preparation crucial to survival. Therefore, it makes sense to present severe weather awareness in an easy to remember format. I encourage and support this principle and I use it as the foundation for my programs. All the instruction in the world will not save one life if people cannot remember what they have learned, especially when dealing with high stress, life—threatening crisis situations.

People react to an immediate, life—threatening crisis situation the way they have been trained to react. Law enforcement agencies learned this lesson the hard way. Many officers were being killed in shooting situations because they were reacting as they were trained. In fact their training scenarios were both confusing and unrealistic. As law enforcement changed their training formats slowly the new tactics produced a more favorable outcome.

The civilian population is vulnerable to the same reaction when faced with a similar life—threatening situation, e.g., a tornado. Therefore, it is obvious severe weather awareness should be instructed in a manner that is concise and easy to remember. For this reason, I recommend simplicity as the foundation for any severe weather awareness program. Long drawn out and elaborate training procedures would be forgotten in an instant, leaving only fear—driven reactions.

My severe weather instruction is centered around two main points. First, the need to know basic tornado survival skills, i.e., where to seek adequate tornado sheltering and alternate sheltering should you be caught away from your shelter; second, a thorough understanding of how your community disseminates severe weather information and warnings to the general public. Adequate shelter is useless unless you know when to take cover, and adequate warning is useless if you have no idea where to seek adequate shelter.

The better we understand tornados and the conditions which are favorable for their development, the better our chances of surviving. In our busy world it is not feasible for us to run and hide every time a severe thunderstorm or tornado watch is issued. But tornados do present an imminent threat to human life and therefore should not be ignored. So the question is, what do we do? The only reasonable solution is to train yourself to be weather conscious. Be aware of changing weather conditions. And know how to protect yourself and others with proper shelter.

Not all communities provide a warning system but the majority of them do. If your community does have a warning system(s), determine which devices you should use to receive emergency information. If your community does not have a warning system there are alternatives. A.M. and F.M. radio stations get up to the minute broadcasts from the National Weather Service and can broadcast considerable distances. When threatening weather conditions exist, monitor the station nearest your location and don't forget to pre-select your best shelter location. The plans you make, right now, can make the difference between life and death later. If you need assistance with your warning or sheltering needs, help is available. The National Weather Service provides various brochures and booklets containing excellent material describing shelter plans and severe weather survival tips. You may also contact your local Emergency Management or Law Enforcement Agency for more information. Assistance is out there. All you have to do is make the effort to find it.

Tornados are spawned from severe thunderstorms where tremendous climatical forces clash together in dynamic proportions. Over the last twenty years I have seen and chased many of them. A spotter or storm chaser should never get any closer than two miles from a twister; however, I have accidentally found myself as close as one hundred yards away from one. This mistake could have cost me my life and worse, I knew better. These killers are not to be chased by a novice or thrill seeker. I must make this point perfectly clear. Only experienced spotters or chasers should attempt to trail or seek out a tornado. The National Weather Service offers spotter courses to organized and authorized groups across the country.

Spotters must first complete a basic spotter course and then, if they wish, they may go on to the intermediate and advanced courses. Before you go out on your own. I recommend a minimum of two years with an experienced spotter. There is a lot to learn from seasoned spotters and a lot to lose if you do not learn well.

Tornado. The very word strikes fear in the hearts of men and for very good reason. Tornados lurk deep inside the dark clouds of severe thunderstorms preceded by severe lightning, crashing thunder, heavy rain and large hail. Tornadic winds can exceed well above the three hundred mile per hour mark inside and around a major tornado vortex, although most tornadic winds fall far short of these kinds of speeds. The Federal Emergency Management Agency (FEMA) says only about nine per cent of the recorded tornado events fall into this category. But don't let these statistics fool you. Even the smallest tornados are dangerous and deadly. In fact, smaller, less powerful tornados can completely destroy a house, or hurl a motor vehicle dozens of feet into the air. Many Americans are killed each storm season by these so-called weak tornados, with winds from seventy-three to one hundred twelve miles per hour. Severe weather awareness does not mean you must become a meteorologists or a structural shelter engineer. But you should be familiar with a few important meteorological terms and you should know the difference between adequate shelter and shelter which does not offer the best protection. The best time to prepare for storm season is before the season arrives, right? Take a few minutes of your time now and evaluate your situation, then take whatever appropriate action you deem necessary. You will be glad you did when the warning sirens wail.

I have been personally involved in chasing tornados and severe thunderstorms for a long time. I have seen the results of massive tornado touchdowns in and around the west central Missouri area. I will never get used to the brutal carnage tornados inflict upon anything or anyone unfortunate enough to be in their way. The primary mission of emergency management agencies is to provide adequate warning *before* a tornado strikes. To accomplish this task takes a great deal of planning and dedication from everyone involved in the organization.

In the wake of a major tornado touchdown survivors are faced with the incredible challenge of putting their lives back together. In many cases what has taken a lifetime to acquire is gone in seconds leaving nothing for the survivor to cling to. Imagine how you would feel if you left your home or business for the weekend and returned to find everything totally gone. Where would you go? Who would you turn to for help? What would you do next? These questions and more are immediately thrust upon a survivor of a devastating tornado. The human suffering is nothing short of a nightmare come true. The traumatic effects of a tornadic event can leave scars in the minds of those who survive. These scars, left untreated, can deepen and threaten both the mental and physical health of the victim for months, or even years following the event. We are just now learning how to cope with such conditions. Critical Stress Management Groups combine professional mental health experts with specially trained peer volunteers to help heal the psychological scars left by such tragedies.

The initial impact occurs immediately following the death or serious injury to loved ones or friends or from major lose of personal property. At first the sensationalism of the moment attracts enormous media attention, and justifiably so. As the events dramatically unfold we often see aid and assistance pour in from neighboring cities, governmental agencies and other groups offering help and goodwill. But eventually, the drama ends. Television, radio, and newspaper reporters pull the plug and return to their perspective homes. The electrifying event slowly fades from the public eye. But for the survivor, the agony of reconstruction and putting his or her life back together again remains a continuing saga for a very long time. Stories of terrifying tornados have been passed on for hundreds of years long before our first settlements in the United States. Many myths evolved with them and many superstitious beliefs were blamed on them. The simple truth is, the tornado is merely a natural phenomenon which occurs when specific climatic ingredients combine to sustain its development and physical properties. It is not a dark evil predator which was sent by God-like demons to punish mankind, as many tribes of American Natives once thought. There are many areas in the

United States where tornados seldom occur or never occur at all. The need still exists to know tornado safety rules. Remember, tornados can occur anywhere, any time the conditions are favorable, even in areas which rarely see their development. However, in geographical areas which are prone to tornadic activity or where they occur on a regular basis, the need to know what to do is paramount to your survival.

I have learned that many people are just as intrigued and fascinated about tornados as I. Why the fascination? Could it be the sheer power of a tornado or could it be the emphasis Hollywood has placed on the awesome beast. I guess there are as many reasons as there are people in the world. But I believe the main reason to study tornados is the fact they are a natural threat to human life. Learning what makes them tick may some day increase warning time. Most people know someone who has been through a tornado experience or has seen movies or read bizarre stories about them. Or perhaps you have heard tales about the unusual and occurrences surrounding them. I feel certain not every tale told about them is true. On the other hand, there are many documented, factual accounts of strange and peculiar incidents left in the wakes of the mighty twisters. Some are quite hard to believe unless you have seen them for yourselves. You will find many such stories, most of which I believe are true, in this book.

Just as people living on the west coast must learn to live with the risk of earthquakes, persons living in areas prone to tornadic activity must also learn to live with that risk. The Storm Prediction Center (SPC), now located in Norman, Oklahoma, is responsible for issuing severe thunderstorm and tornado watches for the entire continental United States. The Storm Predication Center relies on state of the art computer technology and enhanced satellite imagery to identify areas at risk of developing severe thunderstorms. Should conditions exist which favor the development of severe thunderstorms or tornados, SPC meteorologists immediately disseminate the information to the affected area(s). They use several ways to disseminate severe weather information. Teletype, interfaced computer networks and NAtional WArning System (NAWAS). The Center, previously entitled the National Severe Storms Forecast Center, was headquartered in Kansas City, Missouri. When the center relocated to Norman, Oklahoma the center received its new name the SPC.

The early detection and forecasting of severe weather makes it possible for us to continue our daily activities without much interruption, as long as we remain aware of the deteriorating weather conditions. With all the advances made in early warning systems I find it hard to believe many people do not take advantage of the technology. Indeed many people tell me they had no idea severe weather watches had been issued for our area. From my perspective, there is no legitimate reason for this to occur. I believe complacency sometimes overpowers our ability to use good common sense. Today every person should, at the very least, know severe weather has been forecast for their area. Mass radio and television medias provide up to the minute information in a very timely manner. Frequency scanning radio monitors which receive radio transmissions from area police and fire departments are now user friendly and economically priced.

Another good means of staying up to date with the weather is NOAA Weather Radios. They can operate in a silent "monitor mode" which will emit an audible signal when severe weather affects your area. This feature makes them very useful, especially during the nighttime hours when you are asleep. Many areas across the country are in the range of National Weather Service radio towers which transmit to the NOAA Weather Radios. However, you should check with local retailers to see if you live in an area which can receive signals from NOAA Weather Radio transmitters before purchasing the unit.

Persons living in areas which are subject to tornadic development should periodically check the short range weather forecast at least once a day, especially during tornado season. It only takes a few minutes of your time and the forecast usually follows the daily news, which you need to know anyway. During tornado season it is a good habit to check the short range forecast before retiring for the evening.

Unfortunately, there are still too many who choose not to prepare for a tornado. The most common reason is, "I have lived this long without a tornado killing me, and the odds are against my getting killed by a tornado." Undoubtedly these people have never seen the total damage and destruction left in a tornado's path. Don't get caught in this trap. The unadulterated truth is still the same: tornados are a lethal threat to human life. What you do to save yourself is up to you. It's your choice; make the right one.

Over the years hundreds of Missourians have died as a direct result of tornados and thousands of others has been injured. Local governments must deal with the issue each year. Most have learned from the hard lessons of the past and have made preparations for the next one.

Early warning is our best chance of reducing the death toll each year. Emergency Management Agencies (EMAs) have been established to develop emergency plans, coordinate emergency response agencies, and to maintain adequate warning systems. Many Emergency Management Agencies have their own severe weather spotter groups and provide severe weather awareness program instruction. Emergency plans and procedures are updated constantly because they must be ready for use at a moment's notice. For example, in our area, we have placed radio activated tone monitors in all public schools, nursing homes, hospitals, and major factories. We use cable-television override systems to temporarily halt programing to deliver emergency information. We have also installed dozens of outdoor warning sirons.

Emergency response agency personnel sharpen their readiness skills by participating in regularly scheduled disaster drills and rehearsals. A point of fact: our own EMA held a mock tornado drill one month before a giant tornado struck our town in 1977. The drill involved the first area which was struck by the tornado. I will describe this monster in another chapter.

The Midwest and Southern United States record the highest number of tornado events each year. Within this region is a geographical area commonly referred to as'' Tornado Alley." The states of Texas, Oklahoma, Kansas, Arkansas, and Missouri have the dubious honor of hosting more tornados each year than all of our other states combined, although other areas, also known as "tornado alleys," usually support a high number of tornado events each year. However, no matter where you live or what you call it, preparation is the key to survival. The rules do not change from one geographical area to an other.

Meteorology is a complex and highly technical field. Tornado chasers and spotters need to communicate with National Weather Service Meteorologists. Therefore, they must have a working knowledge of frequently used severe weather terms, both technical and slang. Communication between National Weather Service Meteorologists and the spotter or chaser in the field is essential if each is to succeed. Organized chase or spotter groups should take advantage of its array of publications that is available upon request. Indeed, there will always be a need for storm chasers and professional meteorologist. One without the other would reduce the effectiveness of the severe weather warning system. Both storm chasers and the National Weather Service understand the significant contributions each group makes to the other.

Included in my book are some important facts and myths about tornados, various sheltering plans and strategies which you can use to prepare your family for a tornado encounter. Although no shelter, even underground is absolutely 100% fool proof, pre-planned adequate sheltering can dramatically increase your chances of survival. I cannot over emphasis this point enough. Spur of the moment, last ditch efforts to avoid a tornado can be fatal. Pre-planning is extremely important for survival.

There are many questions which come to mind each time I present a severe weather awareness program. Without fail the same questions are asked at each session. I will answer some of these frequently-asked questions and try to clear up many myths or misconceptions about twisters in the following text.

First of all, exactly what is a tornado? According to the National Weather Service a tornado is, *"a violently rotating column of air in contact with the ground and pendant from a thunderstorm (whether or not a condensation funnel is visible to the ground)."* By its very definition, the tornado is nothing more than rotating air in contact with the ground, air which can reach speeds exceeding three hundred miles per hour. You cannot actually see a tornado unless it has taken in debris from the surface or precipitation from the associated thunderstorm. Debris could be anything it comes in contact with, e.g., dirt or pieces of landscaping which have been caught in the updraft. Tornados and funnel clouds are two completely different animals. Too many times the terms are used interchangeably which can cause erroneous tornado warnings to be issued.

So, what is a funnel cloud if it is not the same as a tornado?

The National Weather Service defines a funnel cloud as, " *a violently rotating column of air not in contact with the ground."* Basically speaking, the funnel cloud does not become a tornado until it touches the ground. The funnel cloud gets its name from its shape which resembles a common every day funnel. It usually emerges from a wall cloud, which will be described later. Since a funnel cloud is rotating air aloft detection may not be possible until it takes in precipitation from the parent thunderstorm. Once the funnel cloud takes in condensation it can be seen, it is also sometimes called a condensation funnel. Extreme caution must be exercised when a funnel cloud is observed. Winds from an overhead funnel cloud can do considerable damage to people and property on the ground, even though it does not touch the surface. What might be conceived as a condensation funnel could be a tornado on the ground without the surface observer's knowledge. A quick scan of the horizon may reveal an debris field. I can best describe a debris field as rotating, blowing dust. It is not unusual for a tornado to be undetected until it picks up surface debris, since it is merely rotating air.

A tornado comes from an associated severe thunderstorm. It usually, but not always, forms in the southwestern quadrant of the parent thunderstorm and follows a heavy rain shaft and large damaging hail. Many storm chasers and spotters affectionately refer to this area with the slang term, "the bear's cage." The bear's cage is located in an area known as the "rain free base." The rain free base has little or no precipitation and follows the heavy rain and hail. It is relatively easy to discern the feature from the rest of the thunderstorm. You can see this area best from right angles to the storm. For example, if tornadic thunderstorm is moving from south to north, the best location to view the rain free base would be from the east or west side of the storm. If you attempted to view the storm from the north, you could not see the rain free base through the heavy precipitation which is approaching you.

Where does a tornado or funnel cloud come from?

As I have said the tornado or funnel cloud is formed in the area of the thunderstorm called the rain free base, in the bear's cage. The tornado or funnel cloud develops from another cloud formation called a "wall cloud." A wall cloud is *"an isolated cloud lowing attached to the base of the thunderstorm."* Wall clouds can be one to five miles wide. Most wall clouds rotate counterclockwise in the the United States; however, there have been cases when the wall cloud does not rotate at all. If the wall cloud continues to rotate and visible uplift is present, it can produce a tornado very quickly. The wall cloud must be attached to the parent thunderstorm and usually slopes away from the preceding precipitation area. All wall clouds must be watched extremely closely. If a funnel cloud is to be produced it will most likely form inside this cloud.

Which way does a tornado turn?

In the United States tornados turn counter-clockwise, or cyclonic, the same as the overhead wall cloud. Occasionally clouds will form under the wall cloud and move in the opposite direction, which causes them to turn clockwise, but they are few and far between. Tornados and wall clouds usually turn in the opposite direction in the southern hemisphere. Personally, I really think it is immaterial which way they turn. If they produce a tornado, they are dangerous no matter which way they are turning. Not too many people wait around to see which way the tornado is turning when it is heading their way. Only storm chasers are that crazy.

Why are some tornados red while others are black or white?

Tornados consist of rotating air and ambient air is colorless, right?

As I have said the tornado does not become visible until debris is drawn into the vortex and lifted by the updraft inside. Most red tornados are found in Oklahoma and Kansas, due to the red dirt (or clay) found in these areas. Should you see a tornado from the western side of the thunderstorm, it will usually be light in color because the sun is shining on the vortex. From the eastern side of the same thunderstorm, the tornado may appear to be black or dark blue, since the western sunlight cannot penetrate the mass of clouds and precipitation. But remember, the vortex may not be visible at all if it hasn't taken in any debris which would make it visible to the naked eye. A storm chaser's nightmare occurs when a tornado wraps itself around or inside the preceding rain shaft, making it difficult or impossible for a surface observer to identify it. In this case the best you can do is watch for electrical arching from snapping power lines on the ground and a debris field. This is especially difficult during nighttime chases.

What does a tornado sound like?

The most common sound is similar to that of a freight train or locomotive. From my own experiences I would have to agree, however, the tornado which struck our city in May 1980, produced deafening hissing sound as it passed a few hundreds yards from me. National Weather Service meteorologists told me it really depends on how the rotating winds are interacting with nearby terrain features as well as the strength of the particular tornado. A survivor of the May 1977 tornado told me the tornado (rated at an F4) sounded much like a jumbo jet flying a few feet overhead. A few seconds later the survivor's home was completely destroyed. In any case you should have taken cover by the time the tornado is close enough to hear.

What time during the day do most tornados form?

This question has been asked by many people. According to records from the National Weather Service the most favorable time for the development of tornados is from *5:00 p.m. to 9:00 p.m.* Once the sun goes down the chances of tornadic development decrease dramatically. since the dynamics which support and sustain the severe weather have changed; however, it is always possible that a tornado will form as I have said before: Tornados can strike anywhere, anytime the conditions are favorable for their development.

How were tornados detected in earlier years without weather radar?

In the days before space satellites and weather radars, people had to rely on their knowledge about the weather around them and develop strategies from earlier events which occurred in their area. They simply used common sense. If the weather was threatening they would gather their families and go to the safety of their storm, or root, cellar. As late as the early 1900's there were no weather radars or satellites to give meteorologists an idea of what the next day's weather would bring. The only way people could be warned of an approaching tornado was by telephoning neighbors and family. I have been told many times of how the old ringer-telephone system was used to warn neighbors of approaching storms in our rural area. It was not until the late 1940's following World War II that weather radars were developed.

What are some other names given to tornados? The early Great Plains settlers sometimes called tornados cyclones and dust devils. Some tribes of American Native Indians believed the tornado was sent to earth as a plague by the Great Spirit when he was angered by their actions. Some Indians also believed the tornado would cleanse the land and those who had evil spirits. Australian Natives gave the tornado many different names and for many of the same reasons as the Native Americans. No matter what name was given to the tornado, the end result was the same as today—destruction, injury and death.

When did the National Weather Service began using radars?

The National Weather Service first installed weather radars in the early 1950's. The model WSR-57 weather radar unit was one of the first to be installed, followed by the model WSR-77. Early model radars were developed during the later years of World War II and were primarily used to detect enemy planes, war ships, and submarines. After the war the technology which produced the first radar sets was put to peace time use. The radar system which warned of incoming enemy planes now warned the public of incoming severe thunderstorms and tornados. Once location, intensity, and direction of travel of threatening thunderstorms could be plotted early warning became possible.

Precipitation, in the form of rain or hail, is reflected back to the radar's receiver by powerful radar beams. Meteorologists were trained to recognize and interpret reflected echos on their radar screens. Precipitation which is wrapped around a rotating mesocyclone would reflect a comma shaped return, also known as a classic "hook echo," resulting in a tornado warning for the affected area. These early model radars were the forerunners of today's modern Doppler radars.

Eventually weather radars were installed all across the country. The National Weather Service established zones in each state. Each radar site was responsible for a specific zone within the range of its own particular radar.

Although the weather radars were an effective storm prediction tool, they were not 100% effective. Unfortunately, they could only identify about twenty per cent of the actual tornados which had developed. Surface spotters were responsible for locating all the rest.

I once encountered a tornado which could not be detected on weather radar and I quickly understood why storm chasers performed such an important role in the over all early warning equation. The tornado event occurred on a hot summer afternoon in the mid 1980's. I was sent to a location to observe a severe thunderstorm complex along with storm chasers John Burford and Kenney Mickens. A severe thunderstorm watch had been issued for our area and parts of eastern Kansas. The thunderstorms had not reached severe limits until they entered the county to the east of ours, but we watched as the steering winds moved the individual thunderstorms from east to west.

The thunderstorms had passed through one at a time, one behind the other. We were watching the last one, often referred to by storm chasers as "Tail-End-Charlie." This thunderstorm, unlike the others before it, had a tremendous amount of updraft which pushed the cumulus towers high into the atmosphere. It was apparent this particular storm had the potential to cause us problems. The storm was entering our southwest county area. As it moved eastward I had a good opportunity to observe its back. The heavy lightning and rain was about three miles south of my location. As I watched the rain free base in the rear of the thunderstorm, I saw a definite lowering of the cloud base right behind the heavy rain shaft. After a few minutes the lowered cloud began to rotate. I immediately recognized this cloud formation as a wall cloud. The rotating wall cloud was sucking up other unattached clouds into its updraft. I quickly called John Burford to my location. John looked at the wall cloud and confirmed what I had seen. It was rotating, attached to the parent thunderstorm, and it was in the rain free base, it had all the right parts. The wall cloud was not much over a mile in diameter, but a rotating wall cloud is potentially dangerous and can produce a tornado without notice. John and I radioed Kenney Mickens to confirm what we were observing. Kenney was about five miles to the southwest of our location. He confirmed what John and I saw. We continued to observe the rotating wall cloud. We knew it could produce a funnel cloud at anytime.

We had been watching it for some two minutes when I thought I caught a glimpse of a condensation funnel dart down from the wall cloud. The funnel cloud came down once more. This time John also saw it. The funnel cloud was in the early development stage and would quickly disappear up into the rotating wall cloud then reappear. John and I made radio contact with the other spotter, Ken Mickens. We wanted to be sure before we asked for a tornado warning from our CD director. A second opinion reduced the chance of a mistaken identity. After the funnel cloud was confirmed by the other spotter to our southwest, we immediately notified our Emergency Operations Center. Civil Defense Director, Carroll Uttley, received our report and agreed with our request for a tornado warning for the southern half of Pettis County. As the outdoor warning sirens began to growl, Carroll called the National Weather Service Office in Columbia, Missouri. The radar operator told us we must have been mistaken. His WSR-77 radar was only indicating "garden variety thundershowers" over our area. Carroll asked us to confirm our report a second time. We did as he instructed. The funnel cloud was still there and once more was getting dangerously closer to the surface. The look on John's face told me he was thinking the same thing I was thinking, how could they miss this tornado? After a few more minutes the funnel cloud had stretched its vortex to the ground. No longer a funnel cloud, it had become an official, full fledged tornado. Uttley forwarded the information to the same radar operator and Carroll radioed back in bewilderment. The radar operator seen only moderate rain and maybe, some small hail at the most.

Unfortunately, this "garden variety thundershower" was in fact a tornado with a base of about fifty yards, half the length of a football field. The tornado had already totally destroyed a double-wide trailer home near County Road AA and State Highway 127. The small tornado left the occupant of the trailer home with both legs smashed under debris, nearly killing him. We did not blame the radar operator for his bad call. After all he could only report what he saw on his radar screen. But the incident has always remained in my mind and I guess it always will. From that day on I make it a practice to trust my own instincts and if time permits confirm what I think I saw with another spotter. I don't believe weather radars will ever replace the storm chasers and storm chasers will never replace the weather radars. Perhaps this is the way the system is intended to operate, a checks-and-balance system, if you will. With weather radar providing a constant vigilance over our skies and quality storm chasers watching from the surface, our communities can be reasonably sure of receiving early warning when threatened by severe weather. Storm chasers will always be a crucial part of the severe weather warning scenario.

The National Weather Service realized that they needed a more reliable detection system until new technology could be made available. Meteorologists from the Weather Service were assigned to educate organized spotter groups within their jurisdictions. Part of this training involved the use of common meteorological terms. Terms were selected which insured clear and decisive communication between the weather bureau and the storm chaser in the field. Once the terminology barrier was broken, weather service meteorologists and storm chasers were able to establish a good working relationship? These relationships still oxist today. Even with the newer more advanced radar systems both groups rely on each other's abilities. These trained spotters eventually earned the title of "tornado chasers." Each year the National Weather Service gives their spotter groups refresher course in storm spotting techniques and new updates concerning new technologies and procedures.

What does the National Weather Service use to detect tornados and severe thunderstorms today?

Newly developed technology slowly replaced the older, outdated weather radar systems. A new generation of radars using lightning fast modern computers are now used by the Weather Service using Doppler technology. They are called NEXt Generation RADars, or NEXRAD, WSR-88D's. However, the term Next Generation Radar does not quite fit the present day situation, since they are in use now all across the country. From what I have learned, they do an excellent job. WSR-88D radars still display the location, intensity, and direction the storms are moving; however, the NEXRAD radars go many steps farther. They can indicate rotation deep within the core or a thunderstorm, which indicates cyclonic rotation, necessary to form a tornado. WSR-88D's will display precipitation moving away from the radar site in one color, and precipitation moving towards the radar site in another color. Where these two colors meet indicates strong rotation or circulation of the winds, which in turn indicates a possible tornado. The NEXRAD radars can also detect how close to the ground the rotating winds extend. The new technology of WSR-88D radars greatly enhances life–saving warning time and accuracy, thereby reducing or eliminating the "cry wolf" syndrome.

The National Weather Service also relies on another tool to enhance its forecasting of severe weather. Imagery from orbiting satellites are received at the speed of light, giving today's meteorologists speedy, decisive information about approaching weather systems. All these new tools gives weather service meteorologists the ability to increase their accuracy in forecasting our nations weather. Improvements to the WSR-88D will enhance their abilities even further.

To make any severe weather program work properly, the members of the community must understand the system and how to respond to the emergency information they receive. Emergency Management Agencies and the National Weather Service provide nationwide severe weather awareness and safety programs each year. Educating the public is a never–ending task. To accomplish their mission takes the efforts of many people and countless hours of devoted work. Sedalia and Pettis County Missouri is a community which knows all too well the destructive power of violent tornados. Today, Bill Michael, directs our Emergency Management Agency . Bill and I present a number of severe weather awareness programs each year. Safety briefings are given at public schools, businesses, factories and to the general public. We strive to insure that each person knows what to do should a tornado threaten his or her area. We have found that most people in our area have a good understanding of basic severe weather awareness; however, not every one understands the difference between severe weather watches and warnings. Let's talk about severe weather watches and warnings to clear up any misunderstandings about them.

First, there are the various types of weather–related watches and warnings which are issued by the National Weather Service. For our purposes we will limit our concerns to tornado and severe thunderstorm watches and warnings.

Severe thunderstorm and tornado watches are issued by the Storm Prediction Center (SPC), located in Norman, Oklahoma. Meteorologists there are responsible for issuing severe weather watches for the contiguous continental United States. Watches, issued far in advance of the threat, are designed to give people maximum time to plan their sheltering needs should a warning be issued.

O.K., what is a tornado watch?

A tornado watch means conditions are favorable for the development of tornados in and close to the watch area. Tornado watches are issued for a large geographical area and for extended periods of time. Tornado watch boundaries are usually displayed as rectangular boxes on a map. Most watch boxes are approximately one hundred miles wide and one hundred-forty miles long, although they can be larger or smaller depending upon the location and movement of severe thunderstorms or the suspected area where severe thunderstorms may develop. It is not unusual for tornado watches to be issued when the sky is clear and sunny. Remember tornado watches are issued for extended periods of time and the approaching weather system can be hours away.

Severe thunderstorm watches are issued for extended periods of time and for large geographical areas, just like tornado watches. A severe thunderstorm watch means conditions are favorable for the development of severe thunderstorms in and close to the watch area. These thunderstorms may be capable of producing very heavy rain, large damaging hail, and damaging thunderstorm winds. A thunderstorm is classified as a severe thunderstorm once the surface winds reach 58 miles per hour or it produces hailstorms which are 3/4" in diameter or larger.

Does a severe thunderstorm watch mean there is no risk of a tornado?

Absolutely not. Tornados come from severe thunderstorms. A severe thunderstorm watch indicates conditions are not expected to favor tornadic development, however, severe thunderstorms are dynamic. Conditions can, and often do, change in minutes which can turn the severe thunderstorm into a tornado producer. Always play it safe and prepare for the worse case scenario.

Now that we have talked about severe weather watches it is time to clarify warnings. What is a Tornado Warning?

A tornado warning means a tornado has been spotted in your area, or the probability of a tornado developing is very high. Tornado warnings are issued for small geographical areas and for relatively short periods of time, e.g., usually one hour or less. Tornado warnings are issued by local offices of the National Weather Service located throughout the United States. Tornado warnings are based on information received from two sources. One source is a visual confirmation from surface spotters or storm chasers. The second source is a radar indicated tornado from National Weather Service WSR-88D radars.

With our present day technology it is not uncommon to receive a tornado warning thirty minutes before the tornado has actually developed or touched ground.

What is a severe thunderstorm warning? A severe thunderstorm warning is issued when a severe thunderstorm has been identified in your area, with winds in excess of 58 miles per hour or hailstones 3/4" in diameter, or larger. These reports originate from surface spotters or storm chasers, or have been identified on radar by local offices of the National Weather Service. These warnings typically last a half hour to an hour and are usually for county–sized geographical areas. Severe thunderstorms are not to be taken lightly as their straight line winds can exceed one hundred miles per hour. Hail has been recorded as large as softballs and torrential rains usually accompany these storms. So you can easily see severe thunderstorms can be a threat to human life. Lightning strikes are another dangerous by product of thunder-storms, both severe and non-severe. On average more people are killed by lightning than by tornados.

Perhaps you are familiar with the "F" scale used descriptively by reporters and meteorologists. The "F" is for the person who developed this damage scale, Professor Theodore Fujita, who studied damage from tornados for many years. His scale places a numerical value on damage which is caused by a tornado touchdown . The scale begins at "F0" and ascends to "F5". The following chart shows the Fujita Scale and its "F" ratings.

The Fujita Scale Rating

Type	Wind Speeds in MPH	Damage
F0 Weak	40-72	Light
F1 Weak	73-112	Moderate
F2 Strong	113-157	Considerable
F3 Strong	158-206	Severe
F4 Violent	207-260	Devastating
F5 Violent	261-318	Incredible

A classic example of an F5 tornado is the Jarrell, Texas killer tornado which struck the small town on May 27, 1997, at approximately 3:15 p.m. Much of the town was razed. Only foundations remained in many places where homes, businesses, and other structures once set. Dozens of people were killed even though the National Weather Service Office gave the community 30 minutes of lifesaving warning time, time to get out of the way of the monster F5 tornado or scramble to underground shelter.

Twenty-seven Jarrell, Texas residents lost their lives to this incredibly intense tornado and fifty homes were destroyed. Damages were estimated to be between ten and twenty million dollars. In many areas of the small town only slabs of concrete remained where only minutes before families huddled together in their homes. Nothing was left for most survivors but memories.

Tornados of this magnitude leave very little behind. The tornado which struck Jarrell, Texas was outside the average prime time frame when most tornados form, but again they can form any time, any place the conditions are favorable. There are two words I do not use when referring to weather phenomenon; they are "always" and "never."

As I have already said, tornados can form anywhere at any time; however, they do need a few basic ingredients. Those basic ingredients begin with warm, moisture laden air at the surface, a brisk southernly breeze to add wind shear and cool dry air approaching from the Rocky Mountains or Canada. Then blend in a healthy Jet Stream overhead and mix all ingredients together A tornado is now ready to be born. The dynamics of a tornado are much more complex; however, you get the basic idea.

I would like to share with you some common myths and facts about tornados. First, does raising your windows and opening the doors of your home or business reduce the amount of damage caused by tornados?

The answer is an emphatic, NO, NO, NO. During the early 1970's, the National Weather Service officially instructed the general public to open windows and doors before the tornado struck. They believed opening the doors and windows would equalize the extremely low barometric pressure in the core of the advancing tornado, thus reducing the damage to the structure. This reasoning proved to be totally erroneous.

After years of studying damage and debris left by tornados, and with the advances in the technological arena, the National Weather Service found out the practice of raising windows and opening doors did not make a bit of difference. In fact, people were being killed by tornados while they were opening their doors and windows instead of seeking shelter.

What actually happened was the intense winds of the approaching tornado would push in the facing wall and lift the roof. After the roof collapsed the rest of the remaining walls would fall. The intense winds would do the rest. Opening the doors and windows was only an exercise in futility and in some cases an exercise in fatality.

What actions can be taken to avoid being injured or killed by a tornado?

Let's put it this way. The best and most recommended way to avoid being killed or injured by a tornado is to know in advance where to seek shelter, preferably in a basement or an underground shelter. Most people who are killed and injured are in fact killed and injured by flying debris or missiles. A flying missile can be anything from a piece of shattered glass to an airborne automobile. To survive a tornado you should be below the level of the ferocious winds. Again, the best proven shelter is a basement or storm cellar.

Unfortunately not everyone has access to an underground shelter all the time.

If no underground shelter is available an alternative above ground shelter could be a center room of your home or office restroom without windows, on the lowest floor of the structure. Always place as many walls between you and the approaching tornado as possible. Lie flat on the floor, face down, and cover the back of your neck with a pillow or blanket. If no other protection for your neck is available, interlock your hands behind your neck. If possible lie under a sturdy desk or work bench. Many people have survived tornados by utilizing this kind of make-shift shelter. Don't forget to cover the back of your neck. Again, no above ground shelter can offer the protection of an underground shelter. Many of the people who were killed in the Jarrell, Texas tornado had sought shelter in their homes, above ground, in the best possible locations. But an F5 tornado packing three hundred plus mile per hour wind leaves very little behind. In fact, just foundations, if that. So, if at all possible seek underground shelter if it is available.

What should you do if a tornado warning is issued while you are in a car or motor vehicle?

Some really hard decisions must be made very quickly. The wrong decision could cost you your life. If you know the area where you driving and you know where the tornado is located, very quickly determine if you have enough time to get to a basement. If you do . . . do it, but get there safely. If you do not know where you are and do not know exactly where the tornado is located, abandon your car and seek shelter in a ditch or ravine. A concrete overpass can offer good protection, if you can find one quickly enough. You may also consider concrete barrier and retainer walls. They can offer some protection against the extreme winds and flying debris. Always make as low a target as possible and lie flat, face down, on the downwind side of the wall. Remember, keep the wall between you and the approaching tornado. If you must use a ditch or ravine stay away from overhead power lines. A ravine or ditch may also quickly fill with water. Flash flooding is always a possibility when severe thunderstorms sweep through the area, tornado or not.

If no such structures are immediately available, park your car and exit the vehicle. Do not try to out run the tornado. Some tornados can travel at over seventy miles per hour. Hundreds of people become statistics in this very way. Find a depression in the ground or get behind something sturdy. Again, lie face down and cover the back of your neck. Make as low a target as humanly possible. The depression or sturdy object should not be downwind from where you parked your car or other cars abandoned along the roadway. Motor vehicles are tossed about like toys by even the weakest of tornados; they could roll on top of you. Obviously, this is not the shelter of choice, however, your chances of surviving are much better outside the car than in.

I once watched a tornado stack dozens of cars and trucks against a large utility pole along a major highway in our city. The final pile of motor vehicles was over twenty-five feet high. The interior cars were bent around the pole like horse shoes. The vehicles on the outside were pelted with everything from pebbles to two-by-four pieces of wood from neighboring residences. Luckily no one had stayed in their vehicles opting instead to take shelter in a large water drainage ditch and concrete underpass. Their quick thinking saved their lives. These people had had less than a minute to decide the right course of action. When you are faced with a potential killer tornado your quick actions can make the difference between life and death. Some of the drivers and passengers received some minor to moderate injuries from flying debris, but they are all still alive to tell the tale.

For over twenty-five years I have taught tornado safety to hundreds of different groups ranging from churches, schools and manufacturing plants, to civic organizations and day care services. At each lecture I am simply amazed at the number of families and businesses that still do not have a tornado sheltering plan. In west central Missouri, we are prone to considerable tornado activity. And yet even though our city has been struck four times by major tornados, I still see numerous buildings without a tornado shelter plan. I tell each group, as I previously stated in this chapter, the absolute best time to identify shelter is far in advance of a tornado warning. I also talk about another pre-storm survival technique.

Following the pandemonium of a tornado touchdown, families must have a meeting area, or rendezvous place. These places must be pre- arranged long before the terror begins. Should members of your family or friends be caught away from their shelter area it is imperative you know where you can find them. Be certain each family member, co-worker, or friend, knows exactly where you are to meet following a tornado strike.

If friends and family members survive a tornado touchdown the very worse thing which can happen is not to find each other. The uncertainty which follows such a disaster can induce shock and other medical and mental problems. After experiencing something as destructive as a tornado it is easy to think the worst. I have personally witnesses three such major tornado disasters in my career. In each case, I have found people suffering from severe shock due to their inability to find a husband, wife, or child. Don't put your loved ones through this kind of agony. Be sure each member of your family knows what to do.

Let's use a family of three as an example family and see how they can prepare themselves to survive a tornado. In today's economy it is not uncommon for both mom and dad to work outside the home. Junior goes to elementary school during week days until three o'clock, or so. Mom and dad do not get home until after five o'clock, thus Junior stays with a babysitter or friend until such time the parents can pick him up. Let's say dad works at a local factory which manufactures motor vehicle parts, while mom is a secretary for the local library, miles apart from each other.

As we can readily see, our example family is separated during the day so a common shelter place would not work. Therefore each family member should have a shelter plan at work (and at school), the trip home, and at home. I have listed some possible suggestions for each of the shelter needs. Let's look at a potential shelter for dad.

Where can I seek shelter in a factory or a work place?

In the absence of an underground shelter, dad could seek cover under a sturdy bench or table, away from windows, if possible. He should lie flat on the floor with his head down and cover the back of his neck. He must be aware of potential hazards, especially in factories. Objects which are around him could become flying missiles. A large amount of electricity and natural gas is usually needed in such locations. Following a tornado strike these electrical and gas lines often rupture or become dislodged. Dad should keep a flashlight close to his shelter area to illuminate any potential hazard as he exits the building. He should also know where fire extinguishers and first-aid supplies are kept since he might need them to extinguish a small fire before it becomes out of control or need to stop bleeding from flying debris.

If dad's employer does provide adequate tornado shelter he should know where to go and what route to take. If the shelter plan exists, his employer should post critical information in plain view for all employees and their supervisors to see. If the employer does not have a plan, dad should ask him or her to provide one.

Another possible shelter could be a depression or concrete retainer wall is near the work station. As long dad can keep his body behind a concrete wall, the high winds, flying missiles and debris should blow over him. Before choosing shelter, dad must determine the most probable direction the tornado would be coming from. As dad selects his depression or concrete wall he should place as many walls or heavy obstacles between him and the approaching tornado as possible. Each wall will prevent or reduce the chances of being injured or killed by flying debris and missiles. In any case, he should lie flat on the floor, cover the back of his neck with his hands and make as low a target as possible.

As previously mentioned, dad should also know the location of the nearest first-aid kit. If his employer has not provided a kit, he should ask for one. If he still does not get an adequate kit, he needs to bring his own and keep it handy. Many life threatening injures can be eliminated by simple pressure dressings and bandages. I advise stocking your own first-aid kit yourself, instead purchasing pre-stocked commercial kits. Many items in the pre-stocked kits are not necessary and the items you really need are few in numbers, if they are there at all.

Here is a list of some of the contents I keep in my own first-aid kit you can always add specialty items later.

1.   4' x 4' gauze dressings 10 each
2.   Sanitary napkins 10 each
3.   Roll of bandage tape 1 each
4.   Scissors 1 each
5.   Band-aids 1 box
6.   Triangular bandages 3 each
7.   Antibiotic ointment 1 tube
8.   Flashlight w/spare batteries 1 each
9.   Transistor radio with spare battery 1 each

From my own personal experience, I find first-aid kits such as these are more economical and will most likely stop severe bleeding and dress open wounds far better than mail order kits. You can keep your kit clean by wrapping it in a plastic water proof bag.

Now that we have discussed dad's sheltering needs, lets look at mom's work place. The same basic principles apply to a non factory environment . There are usually fewer hazards lurking about this type of work area; however, pre-planning is just as important, to survive a tornado.

Let's say mom does not have a storm shelter at work. First, we should do a quick survey, checking the immediate area for possible missiles and debris which could cause injury. Aesthetically speaking, large plate glass windows are nice for the employee and patrons of a business; however, they pose a very real threat to human life when tornadic winds turn the glass into miniature missiles, missiles which can reach speeds of over three hundred miles per hour. The main cause of people killed and injured by tornados is attributed to such flying debris. Select a shelter site as far away from any windows as possible.

Next, try to select a room which is located in the center of the structure, again remembering to place as many walls as possible between you and the approaching tornado as you possibly can. The same plan will work for mom as it will for dad. Lie flat on the floor, preferably under a sturdy table, and cover the back of your neck with your hands. It is important to avoid shelter areas which are in or at the end of long hallways. They can become wind tunnels which can thrust flying debris in your direction. Also do not forget the locations of first-aid kits and fire extinguishers.

Many areas are within range of a National Weather Service broadcasting station which broadcast weather information twenty-four hours a day. Included in their programing is a tone activated alert system, in the event severe weather threatens the broadcast area. You can purchase monitors which receive their signals. The monitors are silent unless they are triggered by the alert tone or you can manually activate the monitor to hear the present weather conditions. When the alert tone is activated by the National Weather Service the unit will automatically emit a tone to attract your attention. I have seen such electronic monitors work and provide good first hand information.

Prearranged sheltering for Junior and the babysitter is also a must. Walk through the house with the baby sitter and locate the best possible shelter. See that the baby sitter has a first-aid kit and has a prearranged shelter plan. If you are unsure of the best shelter, call your local Emergency Management Agency, fire department, or law enforcement agency for assistance in choosing the right place.

O.K., mom and dad are driving home from their perspective work locations. There are thunderstorms in the immediate area. Suddenly, a tornado warning is issued. They are in their car, what should they do. Some hard and immediate decisions have to be made. Once again, pre-planning can really help. Mom and dad have to take immediate evasive action to save their own lives and do not have the luxury to start looking for shelter.

Let's walk through this problem. First, each of them needs to identify possible shelter areas on the route to and from work. Trying to out race a tornado is futile. Tornados do not have to follow roads like we do. If a tornado strikes their cars, most likely they would be killed or very seriously injured. It does not take much wind to roll a motor vehicle over or toss it through the air. Don't flirt with death. Get out of the car. If shelter is not immediately available, they should exit and abandon their cars and lie flat in a ditch, depression, or ravine being careful not to seek shelter under overhead wires.

They should also think about their immediate surroundings, especially to their immediate southwest to west. Generally speaking, they would not do well to select a ditch for shelter which is just east of a used car lot, since the tornado would most likely pile vehicles from the car lot on top of them. Some old fashioned "common sense" and preplanning could help save their lives. After the storm has passed and it safe to leave the area, they should meet at the babysitters.

All this sounds simple, however, it is very easy to put off pre-planning until the storm is upon you. Unfortunately, many people have died for this very reason. Don't be a statistic; pre-plan and be prepared.

I have said repeatedly the best all around shelter against the terrifying tornado is an underground shelter. But as good as the underground shelter is, there are still some underground shelters you should not use, such as underground parking garages which have openings at each end that may become wind tunnels.

What hazards should you be aware of which could cause problems with tornado sheltering?

Remember who your enemy is and what it can do to your body. Flying debris such as glass hurtling toward you, lets say two hundred and fifty miles per hour, can cut a person to ribbons in seconds. A basement which has windows on the south or west sides would not be a good place to be during a tornado. There are other hazards to look for as well. Many people hang garden tools, rakes, shovels, and almost anything you can imagine from basement ceilings and walls. The shelter of choice would not include these kinds of potential missiles. On the other hand, if you have a basement such as the one I have described, you can still use it for shelter and be relatively safe during a tornado. It only takes a short time to make yourself a good shelter even if you have a window in your basement.

In fact with a few construction tools and some decent wood, you can construct a barrier shelter in no time. Keep in mind we are not building a blast shelter to shield us against the effects of a thermonuclear bomb. I would start with some good two by four studs, some concrete anchors, a drill and drill bit which is capable of drilling through concrete, wood screws or nails, a hammer. and a few sheets of one inch plywood. You do not have to be an experienced carpenter to complete this task.

The idea is to protect yourself from flying debris as the tornado approaches your home. If you have windows in your basement try to place your barrier shelter in a location where it will not be a direct target of flying glass. First, pick a basement wall for your barrier shelter. Try to put as many walls between your shelter site and basement windows as possible. Chalk mark the approximate size of your shelter on the concrete floor. Drill your holes through your base studs and into the concrete floor. Install your concrete anchors firmly in the concrete floor. Box in your shelter with your two by four studs. Make a small hall entrance into your shelter which does not allow the flying debris to blow in on you directly. Box the walls in with the one inch plywood on both the outside and inside of your shelter. It would probably be a good idea to have your local Emergency Management Agency representative come to your home and take a quick look just to be on the safe side. They will be glad to assist you.

Once you have installed the barrier shelter and had it checked out, place your first aid kit, blankets, flashlight, and transistor radio inside. Once every three months replace the batteries which supply power to the radio and flashlight.

There is one more thing to do which is very important. Tell your neighbors, family, or friends where your barrier shelter is located in the basement. Should your home be struck by a tornado debris could prevent your escape. They need to know your whereabouts to facilitate a quicker rescue.

What do you do if you do not have a basement for shelter?

There are two things you can do to remedy this dilemma. One remedy is to install an outside storm cellar. They are not terribly expensive to construct and offer excellent protection against tornados. They can also be used to store canned goods. Years ago, many early settlers and farmers called them "root cellars." The cellars protected them from the elements and provided a cool place to store their food stuffs. The second remedy is to get to know your neighbors. You might be surprised to find they are enjoyable to talk to and they may have a basement you could share. You might also check with your local churches. Most of them have a basement and may open them during tornado warnings. If you are unable to locate a shelter, contact your local Emergency Management Agency for assistance. Should your area not have an Emergency Management Agency you may contact your local law enforcement agency or fire department. The Federal Emergency Management Agency (FEMA) and your State Emergency Management Agency (SEMA) will provide you brochures and pamphlets upon request.

Chapter Two

Terrible Tornados

Tornado. The very name strikes terror in the minds of most people. For some this terror comes from seeing a tornado face-to-face. For others, film footage from the nightly news captures the agony and pain left in their paths of destruction. From the historical accounts of people all across our country, as well as other countries, we know tornados present a real danger. The National Weather Service maintains records of injuries, property damage, and fatalities from known tornados. Thousands of Americans have died as a direct result of tornados. But today, in an average year, less than one hundred people are killed by U.S. tornados largely due to the availability and use of warning devices. It is imperative to know what means your local Emergency Management Agency utilizes to broadcast emergency information, i.e., tornado warnings, and to know which radio/television station is designated as your local Emergency Alert Station (EAS). Today's modern technology provides us with several inexpensive ways of receiving emergency communications. Take the time to identify what is on the market and how it would best suit your needs before investing in any device. One of the best means of receiving information is through an inexpensive transistor radio, if your area is served by a local media.

Many people have become statistics while in public meeting places. No place is sacred or safe from these monster storms, even our holy churches. When I give my severe weather awareness classes, I refer to a tragic example which left dozens of persons severely injured and dead. A church, in one of our southern states, was in the middle of their Sunday worship services. The weather situation was deteriorating rapidly in their area. While worshiping in their auditorium of their church, a strong tornado developed and made a direct hit upon the unsuspecting congregation. Within seconds dozens of men, women, and children were killed and seriously injured.

I instruct church clergy in our city and county to appoint a responsible person in the congregation to monitor their local radio media in the event of severe weather, especially during tornado and severe thunderstorm watches. This can be accomplished simply with a battery powered transistor radio and an earphone. The person assigned to monitor the local radio station can stay abreast of developing weather situations without causing any disruption to their services.

How far back in our history have we recorded killer tornados?

Tornados have been around for a long, long time. Modern science has made tremendous strides in its ability to accumulate severe weather data, thus improving our understanding in a relatively short period of time; however, attempts to harness and control killer tornados are doomed to failure. Therefore, it is apparent to me we must give the tornado the respect to which it is due and plan our lives around them. I do not believe we should fear them; I do believe we should respect them.

Here are a few of the more famous killer tornados from our past. Natchez, Mississippi. The southern community was the sight of a monster tornado on May 18, 1840. Three hundred and seventeen people were killed that day and scores of others injured. A tonado hit Natchez again in 1908, killing 91 more Mississippians. Then there was the Gainsville, Georgia tornado. Georgia mourned the loss of 203 persons on May 6, 1936. The scars of this tornado would last for many years.

My home state of Missouri has also suffered tremendous tornado related deaths. The oldest recorded killer tornado dates back to April 18, 1880, when Marshfield, Missouri saw 99 citizens die from a huge wedge tornado which cut a half-mile swath through their town. St. Louis, Missouri and East St. Louis, Illinois were hit in 1871 by a killer tornado. Sixteen years later, on May 27, 1896, a killer tornado again struck St. Louis killing 255. But that was not the end. On September 29, 1927 another 72 people died in the rotating winds of "the beast." This tornado, over 600 yards wide, destroyed more than 200 St. Louis blocks. Moving farther south, Poplar Bluff, Missouri lost 98 people the same year from a violent tornado which caught their community completely by surprise. The tornado was over a quarter of a mile wide and stayed on ground for the entire length of the city.

We can not talk about killer tornados without mentioning the most infamous tornado, or tornados, of all recorded history—theTri-State tornado of 1925. This tornado, or family of tornados, killed 689 in Missouri, Illinois, and Indiana. The storm left a trail of death and destruction for 219 miles. Meteorologists and scientists can not fully agree on this deadly event. Some believe the Tri-State Tornado was only one tornado which remained on the ground as it travelled over three states. Others believe the Tri-State tornado was a series of many individual tornados. In either case the end result was the same; hundreds of people died. Raw film footage of this disaster is scanty and hard to come by. I had the opportunity to view a portion of this footage. From what I observed, the message was quite clear. Total and brutal destruction. First hand reports from eye witnesses say the tornado path was up to one mile wide and turned the day to ebony black night. The tornado, or series of tornados, were believed to be in the F4 to F5 range. This determination was made from viewing the debris and destruction which was captured on black and white film by early photographers.

Folklore and personal accounts from Native Americans also include the stories of giant tornados which go back scores of years before the white man arrived in America. The Indians believed that tornados were a spiritual forces which were sent here to clean out the evil spirits which plagued their lives. Some of the Indians actually believed the killer tornados represented the wrath of the Great Spirit, which removed the bad and evil ones from their ranks.

A host of different names have been given to the tornado, among them twisters, cyclones, devil wind, as well as my own name "The Beast." Now that we have identified some of the facts, myths, and history of tornados, I will tell you tornados in West-Central Missouri, and how I became interested in chasing them.

It all began when I was a small child. I would listen to my family and neighbors described the tornado which destroyed the Missouri State Fair which is held in our city. The vivid pictures locked in my memory will stay with me forever. In fact, I was born one month before the killer tornado stuck the State Fair. I do not remember being afraid of severe weather and tornados. Actually, I find them to be spectacular and bigger than life itself. I have learned to respect tornados, not fear them. Over the last few years, I had the opportunity to research the tornado of 1952 and the devastation it left behind at the Missouri State Fair. Here is my account of what occurred on August 21, 1952 which I gathered from local citizens who wish to remain anonymous.

It was a warm muggy Thursday afternoon in our west-central Missouri community. The Missouri State Fair was celebrating its golden anniversary. The city was bustling with thousands of people. Excitement filled the air on the fairgrounds. Livestock and new agricultural implements were on display. Parents and children alike were captivated by the Mile Long Midway attractions provided by the carnival, which had arrived in town by train.

At the same time a cool front was pushing east from the Rocky Mountains in Colorado, making its way across the Great Plains toward Central Missouri. The Fair Director must have felt uneasy feeling the brisk, muggy, south west winds which were blowing across the fair grounds. The warm moist air from the Gulf of Mexico spells trouble when mixed with cool dry air from the slopes of the Rockies. Severe thunderstorms and tornados are the product of such a combination known only too well by people living in and around Tornado Alley, and mid-Missouri was no exception.

By early evening the tell tale signs of approaching severe weather were making their sinister intentions known to those on the fairgrounds. Puffy cumulus clouds began to rise in the distant southwest. Their popcorn looking cloud tops would eventually bring rain, thunder, and howling winds to Sedalia and the Missouri State Fair.

Although sunset was not far off, it was still muggy and hot. The tops of the climbing cumulus clouds began to block out the setting sun. For the first time that day fair visitors had some relief from the scorching August sun. Some side shows and Main Street events begin to close down after the sun had set and darkness fell upon the fairgrounds. There was late entertainment that evening for those who wished to remain on the grounds. The sound of distant rolling thunder entwined with flashes of lightning slowly increased in the south and western skies. The gray clouds of late afternoon and early evening were now full and appeared pitch black. Most of the fair visitors were beginning to be intimidated by the bright bolts of lightning striking the ground on the horizon. Although many people decided to go home or to their motel rooms, I understand that around midnight hundreds of people were still there, most of them relaxing in the many beer gardens on the fairgrounds or enjoying the carnival rides and exhibits.

The steady south winds began to increase, becoming gusty. The wind seemed to signal a warning of approaching trouble as it began to howl and push against the sides of tents and small displays. One Sedalia resident gave me his account of his encounter with the killer tornado.

He began his story by saying he had been at the fair since mid-afternoon. It was getting dark and it was cooler so he decided to walk across the grounds to the swine exhibit. This was around 9:30 p.m. The storm appeared to be moving slowly so he did not think it was going to be a problem.

The gentleman told me he had noticed the lightning in the south and west but he had not heard any weather updates since he had left his home earlier in the day. He said he stayed inside the Swine Pavilion for about an hour or so and then sat down to rest and enjoy a soft drink. Soon it began to look as if bad weather was moving in because the lightning was striking in the distance from the south all the way around to the west of town. He thought it would be best if he started home. He walked through the midway; then walked east to the Grandstands. He then met some friends and decided to sit down inside one of the beer gardens and wait out the storm. He told me later that decision almost cost him and his friends their lives. He said it was a little bit past 1:00 a.m. and the conditions were getting worse by the minute.

The rolling thunder in the distance became louder as it approached the fairgrounds. He said it was as loud as cannon explosions. The wind from the approaching storm consistently increased in speed. The people who had remained on the fairgrounds began disappearing. Some sought the safety of their homes, others crowded into beer gardens and tents. All of them, he said, were hoping to escape the approaching thunderstorm. He said he knew this storm was going to be a bad one, but now it was to late to leave. Now only a small number of people remained. He estimated less than a hundred. Many people, such as vendors and families showing livestock, stayed on the grounds for the entire fair. Immediate severe weather information from the National Weather Service was virtually non-existent in those days. You listened to the forecast on the daily radio programs and drew your own conclusions. The Weather Service had just installed their new weather radars. But getting the word out to the public was another story.

My oldest sister Wanda returned home from a late night date a few minutes past midnight. She and a friend, like many others, had spent the evening hours at the State Fair. She looks back on that night and gives thanks for returning home when she did. For had she remained on the grounds, she, too, could have been injured or worse, become another notch on the tornado's gun stock.

As the storm approached Sedalia, it was obvious to the Fair Director this was no ordinary thunderstorm. But, there were no public address systems to announce emergency information and besides, he had not received a tornado warning from anyone. The tornado took the fair and the city by total surprise. My father Leo Mosier, relying on "gut feelings" from his own personal experiences with the raw power of nature knew something very bad was about to happen. We did not have a basement in our home so all the family could do was wait it out. My father was right.

The time was about 1:30 a.m. The thunderstorm was now bearing down upon the west city limits and the Missouri State Fair. The effects of the thunderstorm were being felt all over the grounds. The high winds from the gust front begin to take its toll on the small quickly-erected out-buildings and tents.

My interview with the elderly Sedalia man continued. "At first the rain fell in small droplets," he said. But within seconds it turned into a deluge of water like he had never seen. Driven by the high winds the rain came inside the beer garden almost parallel with the ground. The rain turned into hail the size of dimes. He said he first became frightened by the storm when he and his friends had to get behind a counter to keep from being hit by the stinging hail stones which quickly grew to the size of golf balls. The sound the hail made as it struck the tin roof and the wooden counter was so loud he had to cover his ears.

Suddenly, the wind, rain, and hail came to an abrupt halt. Silence fell upon the fairgrounds. Many thought the storm was over and exited their make-shift cover. The Sedalia man shook his head "I heard a terrible roaring sound to my south," he said I was still in the beer garden, next to the Midway entrance. It sounded like train rumbling through the fairgrounds from the south but I knew there were no train tracks there. I looked toward the harrowing sound and saw tents and trees being drawn into a swirling dark cloud. Until that time I did not know it was a tornado, but I knew it then. I leaped behind the beer garden building and held on for dear life. The tornado was on the ground for only a few minutes, but, from what I saw, it was enough to wipe out everything in sight. The damage was unbelievable."

One unlucky man was killed from the quarter mile wide twister, and many others suffered injuries from flying debris. Debris from the fair was found as far away as three miles north of the fairgrounds. The State Fair had sixty permanent buildings at the time all of which were damaged or destroyed. The State Veterinary Building was completely destroyed along with a new horse barn which had been constructed for the fair. The bleachers, in front of the Grandstand Stage, was so heavily damaged they had to be demolished. A large number of livestock was also lost to the killer winds. The golden anniversary of the Missouri State Fair was definitely one which would not be forgotten for very long time.

The following morning my brother Richard discovered an abundance of "small treasures" which had been deposited and scattered about town by the tornado. He was proud of them, however, he said most of the stuffed animals from the carnival grounds had to be discarded. They were soaked by the torrential rains and had mildewed. A few homes and businesses had also been damaged by the storm. But the major concentration of near total devastation was confined to the State Fair.

Badly damaged and broken, the Missouri State Fair had to surrender its golden anniversary to the killer

winds. The devastation was the direct result of the estimated 150 plus mile per hour winds. The destruction had
been near total in the hard hit carnival area. "The fairgrounds looked as if a gigantic bomb had been dropped
on it," said one elderly Sedalian. He added, one fatality
was a shame, but after looking at what was left he said it
was miraculous other people were not killed as well.

I interviewed my mother Zelma and learned many of
the town's residents did not know a tornado had devastated their treasured fairgrounds. She told me after my
sister returned home from her date, they retired for the
evening. About one thirty A.M. the terrible storm rumbled
over their home. The walls shook and wind beat upon
the house as if driven by the devil himself. But by an act
of God, the tornado had lifted from the ground once it
savagely devoured the fairgrounds. Only minor damage
was reported north and east of the fair grounds. The city
of Sedalia had been spared this time.

The next morning my father left for work very early,
around 5:00 a.m. My mother did not have their radio
turned on that particular morning since she was outside
the house hanging clothes on the line to dry. She heard
our telephone ringing and ran to answer it. The caller
was my Aunt Mildred, who lived in Benton, Arkansas.
Mildred asked my mother if they had been injured by
the tornado which had struck Sedalia the night before.
Mildred said she had been listening to her radio when
the announcer had told of the terrible tornado which
killed one man and injured others at the Missouri State
Fair. My mother was shocked. After talking with the other
neighbors she learned that none of them knew there had
been a tornado, even though we lived only a few blocks
from where it had touched down.

I had the opportunity to view some amateur photographs of the damaged fair grounds. Despite their poor

quality, the photos revealed major damage to the twisted and bent entertainment rides. The gaily decorated tents, booths, and other displays which were normally scattered about, were gone. Only scattered debris was left where the huge midway had been.

Considering the damage, I believe people at Missouri State Fair were extremely lucky the night of August the 21st. Injuries were called moderate and there was only one fatality. The following year the Missouri State Fair was open for business. What could be salvaged was rebuilt, the rest had to be demolished and reconstructed. From what I could determine it took the remainder of the summer to completely remove all the debris scattered about the grounds. Most of the clean-up work was done by state prisoners from the Missouri Department of Corrections.

The tornado of August, 1952 was an catastrophic natural disaster which will be remembered by Sedalians for many years to come. The risk of another tornado touchdown during the Missouri State Fair is an ever present danger and is always considered each year during the planning phases prior to the annual event. The killer winds of 1952 serve notice to us all. The need to pre-plan sheltering will be just as important in the future as it is today. Emergency planners must keep this in mind when developing emergency response plans. The time of day played a big part in the low fatalities and injuries in the 1952 tornado. I am certain the outcome would not have been as positive had the storm occurred early in the day with thousands of patrons on the grounds. Any emergency plan must be focused upon the worst case scenario to be effective.

I was appointed to the position of Security Force Superintendent for the Missouri State Fair in 1988. The appointment brings with it a large responsibility and I take this position very seriously. The potential for another disaster is always present when you place thousands of people into a 300-acre fairgrounds. You can be sure my emergency plans include severe weather operations and procedures. Although it is impossible to provide sheltering for thousands of fair patrons, early warning can be an effective tool in reducing the number of casualties in such a situation.

Every dark cloud which develops within fifty miles of the fairgrounds receives the full attention of our own radar operator, the National Weather Service, the Sedalia-Pettis County Emergency Management Agency, and our Fair Director, Gary Slater. We all know the fair patrons count on us to provide them with a safe environment to enjoy the fair. We also know we owe then our best efforts to protect them while they visit our fair.

Today we use color weather radar to track thunderstorms and severe weather. We can predict its course and estimated time of arrival from our security office. The National Weather Service Offices in Missouri gives us an extra degree of attention during the fair. At times there are as many as 50,000 people on a 300-acre tract of land. The Missouri State Fair can not afford a tornado to slip in unannounced with that many people in its path. The Sedalia-Pettis County Emergency Management Agency deploys their trained spotters at a moment's notice, should we need their help during the fair. The combination of planning and excellent support during the Missouri State Fair allows us to continue the fun and excitement each year. But I am very aware of what could happen. I pray to God it never does. But if it does we are adequately prepared, to the best of our abilities, to deal with the situation.

It pays to be extra cautious in tornado prone areas during the tornado season. I believe our community is more conscious of severe weather than most in our region since our city has been the target of four major tornados in less than fifty years.

I believe there are many reasons to chase tornados, but by far the most important reason is to give early warning to save lives. Providing this warning is no easy task. Our severe weather spotters spend hundreds of hours learning, watching, and studying the dynamics of tornadic thunderstorms. Trained and experienced volunteers are a vital part of any Emergency Management Agency. There could be no reliable or adequate warning system without their high level of dedication. Meteorologists and storm chasers combine their own specific talents. Storm chasers need the professional expertise of the meteorologist to forecast and identify potential tornados, while the meteorologist needs the storm chaser to verify what he or she is observing on the radars.

In the next chapter of this book I will explain what is necessary to become a tornado spotter. What are some of the tools of the trade? There are many. The first is a quality radio communications network. The need to transmit emergency information to and from a centralized Emergency Operation Center (EOC) is supreme. All the efforts of all the spotters and chasers in the world would be useless if they could not communicate what they see to the National Weather Service or local EOC's. That is why you should never use sub-standard radio equipment. To do so is to put your spotters and community in serious risk.

Access to Doppler Radar is another tool which is a definite plus. Identifying a storm's location and projected course allows spotters to reorganize and reposition to precise locations thus enhancing their surface observational ability. Television and Internet connections can be an affordable and effective way to secure this information. Today's emergency managers have lightning fast access to weather data which ten years ago would have been impossible. Advances in computer technology promise even more technological improvements each year.

Chapter Three

Learning to Chase The Beast

It seemed as if I have always wanted to chase storms. I remember as a small child lying in bed listening to the distant thunder and waiting for the gentle rumbling to become thunderous crashes as the lightning strikes came closer and closer. I also remember stories about the terrible tornado which ripped through the Missouri State Fair one month after I was born. The towering popcorn towers of distant thunderstorms would put my imagination into overtime as the force of the wind bent the willow tree outside the window until it nearly touched the ground. The wonder and awe still remains and I hope it never leaves me.

1967 slowly rolled around and I was nearing my 16th birthday. The state of Missouri allowed teenagers to receive their drivers' licenses at this age. I was excited about getting my license, just like every other teenager. I remember thinking of the new doors which would open once I got my driver's license. But I had one thought which I did not share with my peers: how could I get involved with our local Civil Defense and learn to chase tornados? Then it seemed easy but it proved to be much harder than I had anticipated. A few months before I turned 16, I learned our local Civil Defense Agency was looking for additional storm spotters. They were going to meet on Wednesday evening at seven o'clock and the meeting was open to the public. Meteorologists from the National Weather Service Office in Columbia, Missouri, would teach the course. I wanted to know more about severe weather. This would be a perfect opportunity which I did not want to miss.

I asked my mother if she would drive me to the Pettis County Court House to attend the class. Knowing I was interested in severe weather and tornados and wanted to learn more about them, she agreed. Once there, I saw at least twenty different Civil Defense Volunteers dressed in white shirts and blue slacks. The impressive CD patch on their sleeve caught my eye. Although I was young and did not know much about severe weather, for some reason I did not feel out of place. In fact, I felt very comfortable around the volunteer storm chasers. I stood outside the classroom and listened to the spotters recalling last year's storms and just how close they had come to tornados and severe thunderstorms. Their conversations included words like, wall cloud, gust front, outflow, updraft, and a host of weather terms which I really did not understand. Still I soaked in every word like a sponge.

Three volunteer members immediately stood out fromg the rest. They appeared to be sure of themselves and knew just about everything there was to know about tornados. Over the years my hunch was right, they did

understand tornados and much of what I have learned
about them came from these volunteers. At the time they
did not pay much attention to me but that was fine with
me. I felt honored just to be in their company. I had a
feeling we would become good friends in the future.
Years later we would spend hundreds of hours together
spotting storms and training together.

The classroom was quickly filling up so I decided to
go in and get a good seat. Once inside, we were asked to
sign an attendance roster. I completed all the necessary
information and waited patiently for the program to begin. The Director of the Pettis County Civil Defense
Agency, Jerry Iuchs, introduced himself and his guest meteorologist. The instructor began by telling us the National Weather Service needed dependable and quality
storm chasers to augment their weather radars. I was puzzled to learn the radars could detect only twenty per cent
of the tornados which develop in severe thunderstorms.
The remaining 80% of the tornados had to be located by
surface observers, i.e., our local storm chasers. He showed
us a film on how tornados develop within the severe
thunderstorms and where to look to for them. He also
showed us how we could position ourselves to observe
the storm without putting ourselves in a dangerous position. The instructor used many new terms I had never
heard before. Most of them defined cloud formations
which could indicate the presence of a tornado. I guess
he knew he was talking above some of our heads. He
smiled as he told us not to worry about memorizing all
the terms that night; he had handout material and manu-
als we could study at our own pace. After the lecture was
over I collected all the material I could carry and took it
home to read. I read each pamphlet and manual at least
a dozen times. I memorized each term and cloud formation the instructor had showed us until I knew each one.

From that moment on I could not get enough information about tornados and severe thunderstorms. My desire to learn more about them continues to this very day, thirty years later. A few years down the road I got to know the three storm spotters who had so impressed me. They were Kenneth Mickens, John Burford, and Bill Hill. At every meeting I would learn something new from each one of them. My earlier hunch was right, they were leaders of the group and rightfully so. Later in life they would become my best and most trusted friends.

As I grew older I was able to afford a used citizens band radio. The Agency used CB radio until the early 1980's when they were replaced by more reliable FM-VHF radios. Although I was not a part of the chase team in my earlier years I would listen to them each time they were sent out to chase the severe thunderstorms that rumbled through our area. I was surprised how much I learned by just listening to their radio traffic. When the Civil Defense storm spotters went out to their various locations and began giving their reports, I would try put myself in their places and visualize exactly what they were seeing. Many times I would drive to a hilltop and attempt to locate the cloud formations identified by the spotters. After a while I became fairly good at distinguishing between serious and harmless cloud formations.

After graduating from Smith Cotton High School, in May 1971. I had to make some tough, quick choices. The Viet Nam War was starting to wind down; however the armed forces were still drafting people my age at a frenzied rate. The idea of being drafted and placed whereever they wanted to put you did not appeal to me. I could not afford to attend college which would grant a draft deferment, so I decided to enlist in the regular army as a paratrooper. I figured by enlisting in a crack unit the chances of surviving in Viet Nam would be much better.

I completed the necessary testing and paperwork. Within a few days I was notified I was eligible.

Before signing on the dotted line, I learned the Missouri Army National Guard had an opening. A few positions were available but there were also dozens of other guys my age wanting the positions as well. I decided to give the National Guard a try. I was very lucky. I was selected for one of the four available positions. I remained a member of the Missouri Army National Guard for twenty years, retiring as a Master Sergeant in 1996. I do not regret joining the Army Guard. I had the opportunity to learn leadership skills, emergency search and rescue techniques, plus I had to remain in good physical condition. After returning from basic training, I married and began working at a local factory. Soon I became a father. It did not take long for me to figure out my second love ,chasing tornados, would have to take second place to my new responsibilities. Translated, this meant working many long and hard hours to make ends meet. I went to work for a local manufacturing plant located in the northwest corner of our town. The company made and finished pre-hung veneer doors. I had never worked on an assembly line before, but the job seemed fairly easy and appeared to be a piece of cake; however it did not take long for the monotonous and endless line of pre-hung doors to become out-right drudgery. I have a very real respect for those who make their living in this fashion. It gets tough real fast. I quickly learned the value of "the ten minute break." The job was exhausting and the inside temperature would climb to a sweltering 120 degrees; however the pay was good and so were the benefits. I needed both to support my wife and new born son.

My shift hours were from 3:00 P.M. to 11:00 P.M. Of course, this meant any chance of chasing severe storms was now more remote than ever. I was in a dilemma. And once more, I did not have a clue how to get out of it. I had no choice but to take care of my family, yet I also wanted to be able to chase storms. For a while I had to be satisfied with listening to the storm chasers over the radio. I still kept in touch with some of the spotters but it just wasn't the same. Fortunately, I did manage to make it to an occasional Civil Defense meeting so I could stay current with what was going on. When the spotters went out to chase a storm and I was stuck on the assembly line, I would monitor them on my radio. I was miserable. Really, really, miserable. But I had no choice. Luckily things would change for the better later that year and bring me closer to my real desires.

Spring in heartland brings a renewal of nature and a transformation from bleak winter to lush green trees and meadows. Spring also brings about a change in the weather. The last days of winter struggle to remain and the approaching warmer weather of spring fights for dominance. Whereever the two forces clash huge thunderstorms develop and occasionally produce a deadly tornado. It was on such day that a strong tornado struck a trailer court on the east side of our town. Friday afternoon, April 20, 1973. This day started off like any other. My morning began with a cup of coffee and a quick check of the weather maps and the short range forecast from the Weather Bureau. That day the short range forecast for our area included a high risk of severe weather during the late afternoon and evening hours. After viewing the surface maps it was obvious we risked the chance of tornadic development but of course, I had to work. I brought my portable radio with me to work so I could monitor the spotter group should they be activated later on during the day.

The afternoon dragged on until the sound of the dinner break buzzer stopped the endless flow of doors on our assembly line. The inside temperature was unmerciful that evening. It was a great relief to just sit outside the building in the shade and eat my sack lunch and get away from the intense heat of our assembly line. Once outdoors, I noticed the clouds beginning to gather on the horizon. The puffy white cloud tops were climbing higher and higher. I knew the towering cumulus clouds would soon turn into crashing thunderstorms and once again I would miss an opportunity to chase them.

I turned my potable radio monitor to see if our spotter group was getting geared-up to chase the forming thunderstorms in the southwest. After a few minutes I heard Civil Defense Director, Jerry Iuchs, make an announcement from our Emergency Operations Center (EOC.) The National Severe Storms Forecast Center had issued a tornado watch for our area for the rest of the afternoon and early evening hours. The dinner break was nearly over. I heard the familiar voices of our local storm chasers check in with the EOC, one by one. Not being able to go out and spot the severe weather was torture. I wanted to be out there with them so bad but knew it was impossible. The best I could do was monitor them from my work station inside the sultry factory.

Soon our dinner break was over and it was back to the assembly line. An hour or so crept by. The spotter network began to come alive with spotters reporting severe weather approaching our county. Heavy lighting strikes were being reported in the southwest. The storm was going to be a strong one for sure. I heard Ken Mickens tell the rest of the spotters the approaching storm had produced tornados south and west of our county, which served only to heighten the awareness level of the spotters and me. The storm was breeching our south county line when the Civil Defense Director broke the radio silence with emergency radio traffic. A tornado signature (hook echo) had been spotted by the National Weather Service Office in Columbia, Missouri. The classic "hook" on the radar screen indicated a possible tornado in the huge thunderstorm complex to our south and west. The outdoor warning sirens were activated and the hunt was on.

Suddenly, our assembly line came to an abrupt stop. The normally deafening noises of the machinery left the plant disturbingly quiet. An eerie feeling hit me and I did not like it. Inside the metal sided factory I could not tell what was going on outside. If a tornado struck our plant we would be sitting ducks. Our supervisor began to run up and down the line shouting instructions to us workers. He said to take shelter inside the empty railroad boxcars which ran through our factory for shipping. I really thought this procedure was dangerous but I had no choice in the matter. The boxcars would be hurled around like small toys if we took a direct hit by the approaching tornado. The claps of thunder were becoming more numerous and were definitely getting closer. The flash to bang time was only a second or two making the lightning strikes frightfully close to the factory.

Suddenly and without warning we lost all electrical power. It was dark and quite nerve–racking. On each end of the factory were huge overhead doors. They would be opened to allow the trains to come and go inside the plant and for ventilation in the hot summer time. The railroad tracks ran east and west, providing a perfect wind tunnel for the approaching tornado.

I was really starting to get concerned over this tornado warning. I was in a boxcar, in a wind tunnel (one of the worse places to be in a tornado) and did not have any communication with the storm chasers which meant I did not know where the tornado was located. I must say . . . the situation was not a very pretty one.

In the dark, over one hundred frightened employees inched their way into the parked railroad boxcars. The exterior of the building was built with corrugated aluminum siding. As the winds increased, you could actually see the sides breath in and out with the movement of the metal sheeting. I heard a number of people crying and sobbing while we were in our boxcar shelter. It was a very un-nerving experience, one I would not want to repeat.

The rain began to come down in sheets, pelting the outside of the building. As the lightning bolts illuminated the interior of the factory I would see frightened faces inside the boxcars. Unfortunately I had to leave my radio at my work station so quickly I had forgotten to bring my radio with me. We had no idea what was actually going on outside. All we knew was, the raging weather outside was bringing the tornado closer and closer. Now the steady pelting wind-driven rain on the outside metal siding had a different sound. It was beginning to hail. As the hailstones became larger and larger, the sound of the hail beating on the outside tin siding and roof became deafening. After a while it turned into a steady roar. I knew by all the training I had received that the "bear's cage" would be following the heavy hail and that meant a possible tornado. Now I was getting scared.

We were forced to stay inside the boxcars for what seemed like hours; however, in reality it was only about forty-five minutes. During our time in the shelter of the boxcars we asked each other many questions, questions like if the tornado did strike our plant would the boxcars overturn or be slung like paper in the wind? Would we be crushed by the overhead iron support beams? Would the boxcar shelters actually save our lives. No one really knew what would happen. The best we could do was to hold on, wait, and console each other.

Finally the wind and hail subsided. We were relieved to find the tornado had missed our area. Our lead man on the assembly line told us it was all clear and we could exit the boxcars. Slowly, one hundred scared to death factory workers filed out of the boxcars into the quiet, darkened factory, glad to see each other again in one piece. The afternoon shift supervisor said we were not to return to our work stations as the power was still out and we could all go home early. He also told us the tornado had gone to the south and east of the factory and struck the east side of Sedalia, near the Memorial Airport. For me the news was a big relief. For others it was bad news as they lived on the east side of Sedalia. It was around nine o'clock when we finally were allowed to leave the factory. I quickly went to my work station and retrieved my radio set and exited the building. I was surprised to see a large lake had replaced the parking lot. Some of our cars had actually floated away. The railroad tracks which ran through our building had been washed away and the loosened railroad ties floated around like small boats in a lake. We had received six inches of rain in less than an hour. This deluge of rain will give you some idea of the intensity of the giant thunderstorm which invaded our city.

I walked to where I had parked my car on the parking lot. I had to wad through knee-high water to get to it but a least my car was still there. Once inside, I turned on all my electrical monitoring equipment just in time to hear the radio announcer reviewing what weather events had taken place. He said a large tornado had struck the east side of Sedalia, near the Crestview Trailer Court area, about one mile east of Sedalia's city limits. He also said a friend of mine, News Director for KDRO Radio, John J. Jennings was going to give an on-the-scene report as soon as he could get there. I heard our spotters tracking the tornado as it was exiting our northeast county line. Boone County spotters were now joining in the chase as our spotters were pulled off. Before John J. could get to the scene of the tornado touchdown I heard our other spotters calling in reports of localized flooding and other damage reports from the high winds. I lived in the west-central part of Sedalia at that time and I felt reasonably sure my wife and son was not hurt but I still hurried home to check on them. On the way home I saw that entire trees had been pushed over and their roots pulled from the ground. Also power lines were down just about all over town.

I somehow drove through the high water without drowning out my car. I ran inside and found my family was fine. My wife said she had called our other family members and they too were all right. The actual tornado touchdown was about three miles to the east of us. Since the storm had passed I did not believe I could have been of any assistance to our spotters so I decided to remain at home with my family and monitor the spotter network and local news. KDRO Radio was not a twenty-four-hour-a-day radio station at that time, however the announcer said they would remain on the air until the threat was over. Our spotters in the west area were reporting re-development of thunderstorm activity. More storms were entering our area. I heard the radio announcer say John J. was on the scene near Crestview Trailer Court and he was going to switch to live broadcasting. My friend John J., actually his name was David DeOtt, was usually a calm, focused, and collected news reporter. When he came on air I could tell by the tone of his voice he was observing something which disturbed him greatly. John J. began his report by describing the aftermath of the tornado touchdown. He said over and over again, "It's a holocaust . . . just a holocaust," painting a grim picture in the minds of his audience. After reviewing the damage the next morning, I saw his description of the damage was right on target.

Continuing his report, John said people were running wildly back and forth desperately trying to locate family and friends. Injuries had been reported and people were in route to Bothwell Hospital. But he also said authorities could not rule out the possibility of fatalities; however, due to the intense destruction they would not know exactly how many people were injured until the morning hours. I later learned no one had been killed in the touchdown. Many of the mobile home owners had heeded the warning and ran to shelters or had fled the area before the tornado could catch them inside. The total number of mobile homes destroyed was upwards of 80% of the park. The rest of the city was extremely lucky that evening. If the tornado had changed its course by only a few degrees, the extreme east side of Sedalia would have been flattened. That scenario would have been a catastrophe. Thousands of people live in the east side of our town . . . Even now tears come to my eyes when I think what the outcome could have been that night.

More storms were on the way, so my wife and I decided to stay up. In the stillness of the night we listened to the faint sound of rumbling thunder in the west. We also listened to our radio and scanning monitor. The sound of the distant thunder increased as the new storm cells approached our city. The spotter network was focusing on one particular thunderstorm, as its appearance seemed threatening. We heard one of the spotters indicate the back of the storm had a lowering of the cloud base which indicated a possible wall cloud formation. From the wall cloud funnel clouds and tornados are spawned. A few minutes later the outside warning sirens began to wail. At the same instant the announcer for KDRO Radio

said the National Weather Service had issued another tornado warning for Sedalia and Pettis County. The severe
thunderstorm the spotters had been watching was the cul-
prit. The National Weather Service Office in Columbia,
Missouri had identified a "hook echo" on their radar
screen. We immediately went downstairs to our basement
shelter, bringing our scanner and transistor radio with us.
As we heard the sirens wail in the background a spotter
on the west side of Sedalia saw a rotating funnel cloud
dangling dangerously close over the heart of our city, just
a few blocks from our home. Again the rain pounded outside followed by large hail stones. As quickly as the wind
had picked up it subsided. I knew the funnel cloud was
close by. We waited for the worst to happen but again we
were spared. The funnel never reached the ground. Some
thirty minutes later the radio announcer said the Weather
Service lifted the tornado warning and the all clear
sounded. But our relief was short-lived.

Four times that night the warning sirens blared out
their frightening warning of approaching tornados or rotating funnel clouds. The main damage from the night's
warnings was in fact confined to the Crestview Trailer
Court; however, outlaying communities in our county did
receive damage from tornados or funnel clouds spinning
close to the ground. Injuries were reported in Cole Camp
Missouri a small town south of us. A few farm houses
and outbuildings were also destroyed by tornados that
evening. Overall, our county had survived the rage of severe weather fairly well, with the exception of Crestview
Trailer Court.

The curtain of night slowly turned to daylight. As
soon as I awoke, I drove my car to the ravaged Crestview
Mobile Home Park. I wanted to view the damage left by
the tornado. When I got there I was really startled at the
scene. John J. was right. It looked almost evil or sinister.

Total devastation is the only way you could describe what remained of the once attractive mobile home court. Some mobile homes had been literally ripped into shreds by the relentless winds, while others had been picked up and thrown hundreds of feet into the neighboring corn field. I must say I was also quite confused as well. A few mobile homes were untouched, while just a few feet away an entire home was completely destroyed. I listened to people who had lived in the mobile home court, when they returned from quickly erected shelters in the city, stunned by their words. A woman in her mid-forties tried to describe her plight to a news reporter without breaking into tears. Everything she owned was gone, nothing remained. She could not even locate what was left of her mobile home. She started to sob as she told the reporter she had not been able to afford insurance for her mobile home and she lived on a fixed income, due to illness. She said she had survived the full force of the tornado by leaping from her trailer and crouching low in a ditch.

The woman began shaking and crying, as she told her story. She knew a tornado watch had been issued. She monitored her radio for information. When she heard a tornado warning had been issued she knew she had to leave her home Suddenly she said her trailer began to shake and rock back and forth. The lightning and hail was all around her as she jumped from her back steps to a small ditch. Almost immediately she heard a loud roaring sound, accompanied by a high pitched whistling sound. Then she heard debris being thrown about everywhere, smashing into things. She said it was very hard to breath, as if something were pushing down on her chest. She lay still in the small ditch knowing a tornado was within yards of her, wondering if she would live through this hellish nightmare. Suddenly, she said it all stopped as quickly as it had came. When she raised her head to see what was left of her home, she could not believe her eyes. Only a few minutes earlier she had been relaxing inside her modest mobile home and now it was gone. Just the concrete remained and a few pipes and wires. She then broke into tears and had to leave the area.

I walked to the eastern portion of the mobile home park to observe the damage more closely. What I saw resembled a landfill or dump. A few mobile homes had escaped the fury of the twister. The rest of the homes were either completely gone or completely broken apart, their remains scattered a mile or so to the east and northeast.

The power and destruction of the tornado was much more than I had anticipated. Where the tornado had crossed the asphalt road only mud remained. The tornado had sucked the asphalt up into its vortex leaving a hundred yard gap in the road. The ghostly site remains in my mind to this very day. It seemed impossible that telephone poles and trees could be splintered and hurled hundreds of feet as if without effort. I inspected the damage very closely. I wanted to remember each piece of debris and how it looked. Looking at a ravaged area where a twister has been helps you differentiate straight line wind damage and tornadic damage. This is an important distinction I would need later in my career.

As I left the devastated area my quest for knowledge about tornados became stronger. The Crestview Trailer Court tornado of 1973 gave me a healthy respect for even the smallest tornado. That respect has stayed with me to this day. Should a tornado chaser lacks this respect, sooner or later he or she will become a statistic. Tornados owe no man and will not make allowances for mistakes made by an inexperienced chaser, a thrill seeker, or the person who refuses to heed issued warnings.

Civil Defense Director, Jerry Iuchs, addressed the Pettis County Commission following the Friday night tornado which struck the ill fated Crestview Mobile Home Park. Jerry told them, "We need to develop better plans for opening shelters. Some of these buildings are not adequate, both from the viewpoint of safety and comfort. Also a part time director is desperately needed for this agency." The Civil Defense Director was referring to many of our then designated public tornado shelters, specifically, our Elementary School Buildings. Jerry was especially frustrated when he learned that during one of the tornado warnings on Friday night, one of the schools was not unlocked as planned. Confused and frightened citizens were pushed to near panic levels when they could not get inside to shelter.

After Jerry offered his comments the Superintendent of Schools offered this proposition to the Civil Defense Director. The schools would be unlocked if the Civil Defense Office placed security guards inside the school buildings. That ended the matter. Public shelters were a thing of the past.

Iuchs understood the need to have shelters for the community; however, he met considerable resistance in his efforts to rectify the situation. At that day and time it was common practice to open public buildings for sheltering. Churches also opened their doors to the general public any time the need was there. But public buildings and private churches had to stop this practice due to the rising costs of liability insurance and sheltering became an individual responsibility.

The Civil Defense Agency was forced to approach sheltering in a different manner. A complete paradigm shift had to be made and fairly quickly. A decision was made. If we could no longer offer public sheltering, we would have to educate families and employers to provide for themselves. Not only did the sheltering campaign target the home and work place, the need for sheltering plans for the Sedalia School District had to be included to protect our children while at school. As public sheltering ended families and businesses were forced to devise their own tornado shelter plans.

The Sedalia School Board took their responsibility very seriously. Its emergency shelter plans would be tested four years later, in 1977, when a massive tornado ripped through our town and heavily damaged two of our public schools, both of which were in session when the tornado struck. The tornado drills developed by the school system and the Civil Defense Program, along with a solid spotter network, was credited with saving many childrens' lives that day.

Slowly but surely the Civil Defense Agency received additional assistance and support from the County Commission. A part–time Deputy Director was added to the payroll. This extra help was desperately needed because the responsibilities of the Civil Defense Agency increased each year. The Director was always swamped with severe weather awareness program requests and other such matters, many of which had to be declined since he did not have enough time. The authorization of the Deputy Director position allowed the Director to be much more flexible and allowed more time for training. The Civil Defense Agency continued to improve over the years. Today the State Emergency Management Agency (SEMA) uses our agency as a model for others to follow. We are proud to serve our community and will continue to do so into the future.

Chapter Four

"Black Wednesday"
Tornado on the Ground

May 4, 1977.

The day began much like any other day in mid-Missouri. The mid-morning sky was clear and the sun was shining. The morning weather report promised sunny skies until mid-afternoon. An advancing cold front from the west would increase the risk of thunderstorms for the central Missouri area.

Following the 1973 tornado which leveled the Crestview Trailer Court I decided to enter the emergency services field. It was the most significant decision of my life and I know made the right choice. After careful consideration and a great deal of thought, I decided to become a police officer. The decision to become a law enforcement officer did not sit well with my wife and other family members, but in time they adjusted to the situation. I had

just turned 21 on July 1, 1973 when I applied for a patrol-
man position at the Sedalia Missouri Police Department.
Two months later, on September 14, 1973, I was hired
and went to work. After spending two years on the night
shift, 10:00 p.m. to 6:00 a.m. I was transferred to the afternoon shift, 3:00 p.m. to 11:00 p.m. in the early spring of
1977 and was promoted to the rank of Corporal. My days
off were Wednesday and Thursday.

I was moving closer to my still burning desire to
chase storms as a police officer. I could attend more spotter meetings and had become closer to the Civil Defense
Storm Chasers. The Civil Defense was still using citizen
band radios to communicate. The spotters used the non-
emergency channel to stay in touch with each other when
they were not chasing a storm. I enjoyed the conversations on the radio and made many new friends via the
citizens band radio. As a police officer and an avid storm
chaser, I had the usual compliment of electronic gadgets
and gizmos to fill my off duty vehicle and home: scanning
monitors, citizen band and business band radios, not to
mention barometric pressure gauges, wind direction and
speed devices, and anything else I could get my hands
on. My personal vehicle took on the appearance of something like a porcupine on wheels with all the antennas
and such. One of my monitor antennas had been damaged
and since it was my day off I decided to get a new one.
After two cups of black coffee, I turned on the late morning news to monitor the weather situation. The night before the CB had been alive with chatter. An approaching
cool front would increase the risk of severe thunderstorms in our region the following day. The spotters were
ready long before the storm system began its eastern trek
toward Missouri.

I tuned in to one to our local radio stations to get
the weather. The DJ was just finishing the morning news

report. I knew what had occurred the day before as I had worked late into the night past my regular duty hours. I perked up when I heard the short range forecast, a high probability of severe weather, during the late afternoon. Severe thunderstorms, large hail, and the possibility of tornados existed in our area. I called my family members to make sure they knew about the expected severe weather. The best time to prepare for tornados is before they occur. My wife, Marcia, worked at our local hospital as a nurse. It was her day off as well. This meant my son, Ronnie, would be at home and not at the baby sitters.

Morning quickly turned into early afternoon and I had not repaired the antenna on my car. I knew I would need it later when the storms begin to break out. The afternoon heating and the increasing humidity spelled trouble. The approaching cool front would undercut the warm muggy air and force developing thunderstorms high into the atmosphere. The already brisk south winds were getting stronger, adding fuel to fire. A tornado watch was issued for our area by the National Severe Storms Forecast Center, in Kansas City, Missouri. The tornado watch did not surprise any of the Civil Defense spotters. The Civil Defense Communications Network was activated which instigated immediate responses from the spotter group. The Civil Defense Director, Jerry Iuchs, began assigning spotter locations and checking them in as they came up on the air. I advised the Emergency Operations Center (EOC) I would go out after I replaced the antenna on my car. It was nearing three o'clock and the skies were beginning to darken significantly. My family and I drove to one of our shopping centers to buy a replacement monitor antenna. We monitored the severe weather situation in our car. Information on the radio net indicated strong thunderstorms were approaching from the southwest which forced a quick antenna purchase and installation.

We had just left the shopping center when Director Orendorf advised us of a sobering situation. The National Weather Service Office in Columbia, Missouri, was observing a "suspicious echo" on their weather radar screen. The area under suspicion was approximately fifteen miles to our southwest, in the northeast corner of neighboring Henry County. The cloud tops to the southwest were high in the atmosphere reaching well over fifty thousand feet. It was obvious to me this storm meant business. The sun was shinning on the very tops of the main storm towers making them white as snow, but miles below the tops of the thunderstorm the base of the clouds had turned black as night. I told my wife I thought it would be a good idea for them to remain at the police department since we did not have a basement in our home at that time. I would go out with the spotters. The radio net was fairly quiet now. That is typical when a possible tornado is lurking near by. We keep the net clear for emergency traffic. We were just a few blocks from the police department. when we heard one of the spotters, the Reverend Greg Hibbard, call the police department and order them to sound the outdoor warning sirens. Columbia weather service office had issued a tornado warning for Sedalia and Pettis County. A large tornado was approaching from the southwest, less than a mile away from the southwest city limits. His voice had a near panic tone. If the tornado continued its present course a major sub-division would be in its path. He frantically repeated his request to activate the outdoor warning sirens. There was no time to spare as school would soon be letting out and the children could be caught outside or in the busses.

Staff Writer, Ed Vaughan, of the Sedalia Democrat Newspaper interviewed Civil Defense member Greg Hibbard following the tornado touchdown and gave this report. Greg was credited with saving hundreds of lives by ordering the outdoor warning sirens to be activated before he actually saw the tornado. That early warning made the difference between life and death. "Actually if I had gone by the book I wouldn't have hit it (the Civil Defense warning sirens) so soon, but Columbia Weather had told us there was a possible tornado by Greenridge so I hit it. If it hadn't been a tornado I would have been accused of crying wolf." I told my wife to take our son downstairs and stay there until the all clear was given. The outdoor warning sirens began to wail, demanding immediate attention and response. The wailing of the warning sirens and major tornado knocking at your door will make your blood run cold. The southern sky was black as coal with constant bright flashes of ground to ground lightning. The sirens continued to blow while the thunder crashes came closer and closer. All we could do was wait for the inevitable onslaught to come.

Our Police Chief, Bill Miller, met me at the front door. The chief ushered my family and the other Municipal Building employees to the basement of the police department. The door swung open and in came officers Tom Wood and Hal Purdue. All of us were in civilian clothes. The Chief told us he believed the tornado would smash through the Southwest Village sub-division. If it did, he said, the potential for fatalities would be great. The chief ordered us to the back door to watch for the approaching tornado. The projected patch would bring it dangerously close to our headquarters. We were ordered to keep the back door open to reduce the barometric pressure (an action we now know is a no-no) to lessen the damage to the building if the tornado were to strike it. Man, talk about a rough assignment. We did as we were told, but we did not like it.

The chief returned to the back door where we were stationed. He told us from all indications, much of Southwest Village had already been destroyed. I could not believe what he was saying. I had patrolled the peaceful sub-division just a few hours before. Surely his information was incorrect, someone must have made a mistake. We pinned our badges to the outside of our shirts as we heard the reports coming in for ourselves. It just kept getting worse by the minute. As we glued our eyes to the southwest we soon began to see debris flying up into the air around the twister which was now less than three blocks from the back door of our police station. Soon we could identify parts of houses, roofs, trees, and other pieces of debris, were all spiraling inward and upwards toward the sky. The funnel shaped cloud was enormous and was cloaked in emerald green and dark blue directly behind the immense rain shaft. As the debris field edged closer to us, the thick spinning mass revealed the vortex of the storm which had now turned dark blue. It must have been a quarter of a mile wide. On the very outside of the tornado everything appeared to be moving in slow motion. But in the core of the brutal tornado wind speeds were spiraling at over two hundred miles per hour.

The tornado made an unmistakable "hissing" sound as it approached, followed by a tremendous deafening roar. The ground felt as if it were shaking and it became very hard to breath. All of this was happening way too fast to fully comprehend. I could not believe what I was seeing. The overwhelming mass destruction continued northeast. Hal and I could tell the tornado was nearing the Mark Twain elementary school. We did not know it at the time but the tornado had already ravaged the Horace Mann elementary school a little over a mile away.

The Mark Twain was being destroyed right before our very eyes, just beyond the row of houses to our west. It was a sight I will never forget. We hoped and prayed the children were in a safe place. The tornado proceeded on its way, tracking northeast with a ground speed of thirty-five miles per hour hammering everything in its path.

Then suddenly large pieces of debris began falling all around us. Large pieces of construction material, trees and other large pieces which I could not identify. The vortex was now obscured in the rain shaft ahead of it. I was nearly in shock. How could a disaster of this proportion come and go so quickly. The entire life of the tornado was only some twenty odd minutes but for Hal and me it was an eternity. I feared the worse. Surely we would have many injuries and deaths from this rotating nightmare. Arcing electrical lines were popping like the fourth of July hideously marking the progress of the tornado which was still on the ground and maintaining its strength and power. As the monster slowly edged its way from the heart of our city I could hear dozens of sirens. Police, fire, and ambulance units scrambled in behind the tornado to handle the emergency situations left in its path.

We received terrifying information over our radio system. The violence of the storm had destroyed much more than any of us imagined. Only by a small miracle had it missed our police headquarters skirting by only a few blocks away. Breathing a short sigh of relief we monitored the radio traffic of our officers and other emergency response agencies. All the on-duty uniformed officers were desperately trying to radio critical information to our dispatcher. Unfortunately, they were all trying to talk at same time, thus only distorted radio signals were being received. The first few minutes following a disaster of this proportion is always chaotic and unorganized but quickly settles down. Chief Miller called Hal and me to his office. He had returned from the communications center with dreadful information. The tornado had cut a path of destruction right through the middle of the city. Chief Miller told me to to get Officer Tom Woods and Hal Perdue and proceed directly to Southwest Village. He said the large upper middle class sub-division had been heavily hit. I was to organize a command post and begin operations until I could be relieved at a later time. I told the Chief I would do my best, but in the back of my mind I felt apprehension and uncertainty. I had been a supervisor for less than a year and was now facing a major disaster command. What would I do and how would I do it. How much of the area had been destroyed? How many casualties were there? This was a huge load for a young, twenty-four year old corporal. I offered a quick prayer and mustered enough courage to meet the challenge which lay ahead. We removed the debris on the windshield, then with red lights flashing and our siren screaming, we took off for our assignment .

The early warning provided by our spotter network had saved many lives that day. Forty people were injured and treated at our local hospital, with only five considered as seriously injured. Damaged or totally destroyed in less than twenty minutes were: 1700 homes, 1400 automobiles, two schools and 21 mobile homes; 1800 homes were left without telephone and/or electrical service. The total estimated loss was set at $19 million. The damage totals were astronomical and it would take a monumental effort to recover. When it was all said and done it had taken many months and in some cases, years to recover. Some decided it was not worth the effort and simply moved away but most stuck it out to the end.

In route to our assignment we could see some areas in town had been spared, but as we neared the path of the twister it became impossible to get through the debris on the roadway. I decided to drive west on U.S. Highway 50 to Highway 65, then south to Southwest Village. The collection of scattered objects in the road was getting worse each block we traveled. I remember the look Hal's and Tom's eyes when we approached Grand Ave and Highway 50. The scene was incredible. Huge trees were uprooted and scattered everywhere leaving cavernous holes. Blinding arcs of electricity from downed power lines littered the roads and sidewalks all around us. Overturned motor vehicles were scattered about like toys, many of them piled on top of each other. Obviously we could go no further west on Highway 50.

We searched for an opening. Our diligence was rewarded with a make-shift path across some front lawns which only moments before had been beautifully maintained and manicured. We made our south turn onto Grand Avenue and then a right turn from Grand onto Sixteenth Street and headed west. The further west we drove the more debris we saw. The roads were becoming impassable. I remember wondering about the kids when the tornado hit Mark Twain School and I was suddenly jolted by another hideous thought. The Horace Mann Elementary School was just ahead and by the looks of things this area had been hit just as hard. Horace Mann School had most likely been in the path of the tornado as well. I advised the two officers we would quickly check out the school on the way to Southwest Village. They were as distressed over the possibility of injured kids as I. My nephew, Kevin, attended the school which did not make things any easier for me.

This scene as we made our way to the school building was ghastly. Some of the houses near the school had been severely damaged and were on fire from the ruptured natural gas lines. One house across the street from the school building was burning. Some of the motor vehicles in the area had been overturned and smashed into others. Some of the battered cars had two by four boards stuck through them. But that was not the worst sight.

The tornado had hit the school. The nightmarish view of broken and twisted structural material was beyond my comprehension. The roof was missing and bricks were piled and thrown about. The windows were either missing or broken. More motor vehicles were pilled on top of each other as if they had been placed there by a crane. I noticed the U.S. flag was still flying although not much was left of it as it had been tattered from the terrific winds. It reminded me of a war movie. I knew hundreds of school children could be casualties as well as dozens of school teachers, custodians, and support personnel. We had to stop and determine just how bad they had been hit.

When we pulled up a school teacher slowly approached. She was soaked and her clothing was soiled and torn. She told us the children had suffered only minor injuries from the storm, none of them was serious. She appeared to be in mild shock but did not seem to require any immediate medical care. We told her help would be on the way as soon as possible. The information helped somewhat to ease our fears. At least none of the kids were seriously hurt or killed. I had never seen such damage of this scale before, neither had Hal or Tom. Our department was already overloaded and overwhelmed and we had only been into the disaster five minutes. I was convinced this was going to be the challenge of my lifetime and I had to be ready. I did not have a choice. Officer Woods reported what we had learned to our police radio operator. Getting on the radio was a major accomplishment in itself. Hundreds of damage reports, ambulance and fire department requests were pouring in. We still had no real idea just how badly the tornado had damaged Southwest Village or the rest of the city for that matter. We had to press on but I was not able to get through all the debris. Entire trees lay across the road accented by an upside down car here and there, not to mention the hot power lines arcing all around us.

As I slowly inched my way through the maze of debris, Officer Woods tried to get back on the radio to order fire fighting equipment to the area. Some of the home owners were using water hoses to fight the blazes. Dozens of people were milling about looking as if they were lost or in shock. After many attempts, Tom finally got through to the radio operator. She replied all of the fire units were already deployed but she would send the next available truck that way. The radio operator had to prioritize each call for help and maintain a waiting list. I did not envy her job. It had to be tough. Tom also asked for ambulances and rescue personnel to report to the school. The dispatcher said it would be some time, but she would send assistance. This situation had already turned into a nightmare and we had hardly just begun.

After driving my squad car over small trees, parts of buildings, roofing, and everything in between, we proceeded west on Sixteenth Street and we made a left turn onto U.S. Highway 65. The roadway was fairly clear at that particular location. The tornado had traveled just east of there and we could now increase our speed without damaging our car. But only six blocks south of Sixteenth Street and U.S. Highway 65 we ran into a real problem. Huge utility poles lay across the four lane highway. We had already seen buildings and homes nearly destroyed but I could not quite comprehend how heavy buildings, made of brick, had completely disappeared. Dozens of cars which had not been pillaged by the tornado were parked haphazardly along and in the Highway. The drivers of the vehicles were gone. It was nearly impossible to get around the downed utility poles and motor vehicles.

I topped a small hill, next to the Missouri State Fair Grounds. Ahead was an even more shocking view than we had seen at Horace Mann Elementary School. Most of the structures from the 2200 block of South Highway 65 (Limit Ave.) were gone, any building which remained was severely damaged. Only the foundations remained on many. Beside the arcing of electrical wires, huge streams of water were spraying from plumbing fixtures, which just minutes before had been ripped away from the walls and floors of the doomed buildings.

The stretch of highway did not resemble anything I had ever witnessed before. We could only drive at a snails pace. Debris was everywhere. We crept south to the MK & T railroad underpass. To our right was the State Highway Barns now only a shell of the structure. Across the street, the Jockey Club Lounge was gone, completely gone! Only the pool table remained in the middle of the floor. Later I learned someone in the lounge had crawled underneath the pool table when the roof was pulled away by the tornado. Remarkably he had survived with only minor injures. I saw stacks of cars and trucks, piled near 25 feet high against one of the utility poles which survived the ravaging winds. One car was entirely wrapped around and suspended from the huge utility pole, about 25 feet in the air. We were devastated. How many bodies would we find under all this rubble? How many people had actually survived? Could we handle this catastrophe of this size? Did we have what it takes to endure this carnage? After reporting what we had seen, we continued by using my squad car as a combination battering ram and bull-dozer. After quite an ordeal and some wasted time, we were able to drive south toward our goal, Southwest Village. As our siren wailed, I remember asking Tom if the old Country Club-Club House was still there. It was surrounded by a manicured nine hole golf course and was the center attraction for the upper class. I hoped it survived. My hopes were soon shattered as we approached the Country Club. "My God. . . it's gone!" Rodney exclaimed. The Pro-Shop, the Club House, the Pro-Golf Course, everything gone. All the magnificent trees were twisted off or violently up-rooted. The once picturesque scene was had totally vanished except for a huge pile of rubble.

The sights and sounds, up to now were horribly unbelievable. What would Southwest Village look like? A few seconds later we had the answer. Southwest Village appeared over the horizon as a hellish apparition. We stared at huge holes where homes worth hundreds of thousands of dollars should have been nestling under towering trees. Dozens of others were just flattened. I told Tom to report what we seen. I don't believe I could have! I drove past the Best Western Motel, south to Southwest Village. All around us homes were missing, collapsed, or heavily damaged. Yet, other houses sitting next door to these appeared to be undisturbed. I stopped my patrol car near a large assembly of dazed citizens. Around us, homeowners and neighbors were running about trying to find loved ones or friends. Most were bleeding, their clothing torn or missing; some were even half dressed. All were scared.

Running in emergency mode, we normally could have made the trip to Southwest Village in five or six minutes. Our trip from the station took almost 25 minutes. I told the police radio operator we were on scene and the situation was bad. I also told her we were going to establish a command post at Southwest Village and

Wing Ave. The radio operator acknowledged our broad-cast. I told her we would report in when we accessed the situation somewhat further. By the look on the faces of the victims around us I knew we must establish control and maintain some resemblance of law and order. If we displayed the slightest hint of uncertainty or gave the appearance of being frightened ourselves they would most surely panic and take matters into their own hands. In reality, I did not have a clue where to start, however, I knew not to show it. Hal and Rodney gave the same appearance of control, but I knew they were just as perplexed and unsure of the immediate future as I was.

We did not know it at the time, but it would be three days before we would finally rest and get some much–needed sleep. During the ordeal, I learned you can do anything if you have no other choice. To this very day, I do not know how we continued for three and a half days without sleep. My medical friends tell me adrenalin, fear, and the fight or flight syndrome, can drive a person way past their normal limits. I guess they are right. I don't know for sure what kept us going but, I'm thankful it did.

The first major hurdle was obvious. We had to establish a consolidated command to coordinate search and rescue efforts. The term "Incident Command" did not exist, at the time. We practiced the system but we did not have a name for it. The way we assembled fire fighting, emergency medical, search and rescue, and law enforcement vehicles, was one and the same. We needed help and a lot of it. But the police radio operator could not get us any additional assistance. She could only give us the same promise . . . when it is available. The flattened sub-division was in desperate need of help, and we had to provide it. I knew that we would be receiving help from the Missouri State Highway Patrol and other agencies in and around our area. The question was when? I also had an immediate situation which I had no answer. How many other emergency response agencies were already in Southwest Village and how much personnel did they have with them?

Communication was very poor in the early 1970's. Our department only had a limited number of walkie talkies. We now have individual portable radios which have multi-channel capabilities, but not then. Eventually, a few firemen from the Sedalia Fire Department joined us in Southwest Village. Historically, the Sedalia Fire Department and Police Department had always competed with each other in a healthy way. This time, we worked together side-by-side without the jokes and ribbing. But we were still critically short of manpower and equipment. We did not have enough personnel to even think about search and rescue missions, but they were desperately needed.

Multitudes of people began to arrive in the Southwest Village area. I did not have adequate security to establish a perimeter to keep sight seekers out. I was not sure the growing number of people actually lived in the area, if they were looters, or if they were there to lend assistance. We had to assume they were there to help, until adequate manpower arrived. I was beginning to think it was hopeless. Many questions were whirling about my mind at one time. Were there injured or dead victims lying under the tons of rubble and debris? If so, how were we going to get them out? To complicate the matter, how would we get the injured victims to medical assistance, once we extricated them? A supervisor's nightmare, that was my view of the situation. What a dilemma! We needed search teams, emergency medical units, supporting law enforcement and fire fighting units from other agencies, and able citizens to assist us with search and rescue and I needed them all now. All local ambulances were taxed beyond their means. I knew it would be quite some time before other officers would arrive. For the first time that day it hit me . . . right square in the face. I was scared to death. I had never felt so alone in all my life.

Scores of people continue to approach us for help. Each one demanding top priority. I knew any decision would be much better than no decision. I decided the first priority would encompass the transporting of known injured victims to the hospital for treatment. Officers Perdue and Woods told the crowd our plan. The civilian rescuers were told to bring the walking wounded to us. If the other wounded could not be moved, come back to our command post and we would get them help. I did not how we would could get the most severely injured victims professional help. Until it arrived all I could do was use more civilians who wanted to help. The directions we gave seemed to please the crowd, at least for the time being. Many of the people around us who were not injured or in shock offered their help. Mid-Missourian's are know for their willingness to band together when the chips are down and boy were the chips down. This help was definitely welcomed. I had made it so far. They were helping us, instead of fighting us, a definite plus.

We began to assemble the injured and sent the good Samaritans with the injured to the hospital. But search and rescue would have to wait until more help arrived.

After a few more minutes I was relieved to see a Sedalia Fire Truck, with six personnel on board, turn the corner. I met with the Fire Department official in charge. Our command post, now consisted of a fire truck and police car. Not much; however we were at least getting organized. The Fire and Police Departments were working together, doing the best they could under the circumstances. Wing Street Command Post was now operational.

The Fire Department Commanders and I made urgent requests for assistance from our respective departments but, they could not send help they did not have. We would have to wait until Mutual Aid assistance from other cities and counties arrived.

As more firemen and police officers arrived from off duty status we implemented the second phase of our plan, an organized search and rescue mission. We organized search areas by using the existing streets for grids, searching east to west. All the structure fires were now apparently out which left the fire department available for rescue missions. We divided into three man search teams and searched house to house, an effective way to be sure we did not miss anything or any body. We divided into three man search teams. Each team was assigned a street. The search and rescue missions took the rest of the daylight hours. Before we began our missions the police radio operator received information the Army National Guard would be arriving soon. Mustering their troops can take considerable time. Again, I breathed another sigh of relief. I fully understood our resources were already exhausted. The hundreds of damaged businesses and homes could not be protected by our department alone, and I knew it. Looters would creep out as soon as the night fall arrived. The Missouri Army National Guard and the Missouri State Highway Patrol would ease our stretched resources.

The first house Officers Perdue, Woods and I searched in our sector was a large, ranch style home. The south walls were pushed in and the roof had collapsed on top of the southern wall and appeared to have collapsed all the way down to the basement. Outside the house we found a woman standing beside a demolished vehicle. She was definitely in a state of shock. She was violently shaking and crying. She grabbed us as we approached her and said one of her family members was inside the house when the tornado swept through. Officer Perdue reassured her and turned her over to her a neighbor to calm her.

The house was a total wreck. The roof was where the bottom floor should have been. We frantically searched for a way in but the huge pile of debris made it difficult to determine how to get down inside. After a few minutes of searching, I finally found a tunnel–like hole in the rubble. Hal and Rodney helped me slowly worm myself into the tunnel. I found a way to what I believed was the basement of the now demolished home. But the tunnel quickly disappeared.

By moving one board at a time I was able to slowly inch forward and downward and worked my way to the basement floor. The entire roof was just inches from the top of my head. I looked under what was left of the bar, the heavy tables and furniture, anywhere which might have served as a make-shift shelter where the man could have been. I could not find him. I was afraid he was under all the boards and material I had crawled through to get inside. I yelled to Tom and Hal and told them I had no luck finding the man. I was relieved to hear Officer Wood yelling back to me. He said the woman had found her husband outside the house, in some rubble. The next task was to get out the same way I had got in. Not as easy as it sounds.

I finally relocated the tunnel which had led me into the basement. I was about half way out when the roof began to shake and creak loudly. I decided it was time to get out of there. Now! Before I could completely remove myself from the rubble, the roof collapsed again. After the dust settled I looked around to see if I was trapped. But actually, the collapse of the roof had made the tunnel larger. I was able to exit the tunnel without further problems, though I had to push my way out with my feet, to make the final few yards. Perdue and Woods helped pull me out. I was so glad to get out of the dirt and grime, I didn't notice the six inch nail which had penetrated the bottom of my right tennis shoe and exited the top of my foot. Hal and Rodney removed the nail. Things being what they were, I continued on without giving the wound a second thought. It must have been mind over matter. If you don't mind, it doesn't matter!

We searched at least thirty homes in our search area and we combed through countless numbers of twisted and bent motor vehicles, as well. With every discovery of a child's toy or doll, our hearts would skip a beat, or so it seemed. With God's help, we never found a child injured. We systematically sifted through enough debris to last a lifetime. The unbelievable amount of rubble appeared to be endless. Even the most experienced search and rescue personnel would have been challenged by the near total devastation in the Southwest Village area. There were more houses damaged or destroyed than were left untouched.

We were nearing the end of our search area when Tom found a woman, in her sixties, with her clothing ripped to shreds. Luck was with her that day as she was only suffering from superficial wounds. The bleeding had stopped but it was apparent she was in shock. One minute she would be screaming as loud as her lungs would allow, the next moment she stared ahead blankly. Officer Woods desperately tried to calm her without success. She repeated this cycle numerous times. We knew she was desperate need of medical help; unfortunately, we had none at the time.

Finally, she stopped screaming and almost instantly seemed to gain her composure. She began to sob and point to a totally destroyed car, wrapped neatly in the top of a large tree. She told us her husband was inside the car when the tornado struck. She had seen the vortex approaching, just a few yards away, and made it to what was left of her home for shelter. To this day I can not tell you what type or make of car it was. I only know it was a dark color. Not much was left. We had to climb up and into the car to investigate. We checked the car the best we could. He was not inside. We could tell by her face she was ready to slip back into shock, when we did not locate her husband. Then unexpectedly her husband appeared from behind a demolished neighbor's home. He too was only slightly injured. He had seen the tornado coming and had run to the neighbor's house for cover, as it was closer than his own home at the time.

We finished our assignment, then went back over the area. It appeared all the injured had been treated and to the best of our knowledge everyone had now been accounted for in our assigned search area. We made it back to the command post both mentally and physically exhausted. At the command post, we were met by one of our senior sergeants. He gathered Perdue, Woods, and me along with some other Sedalia police officers and said we were needed for search and rescue in the north central portion of the city. The area had been hit hard as well and they needed more help. On the way to the other devastated area, the radio operator contacted our sergeant. She wanted us to go to yet another area. The Country Club Edition had also fallen victim to the tornado and had heavy damage. The edition was close by. We arrived at the corner of Honeysuckle and Country Club Boulevard. My brother Richard and his wife Doris had lived in a house in the sub-division and had just recently moved out. From what I saw it was a good thing they moved when they did.

What I saw when I looked in the direction of my brother's old house momentarily made me believe I was disorientated. I could not find it. It was totally gone. The only thing which remained was a bathroom stool and a hall closet. I asked a neighbor if the people who owned the house had made it. The neighbor told me one of the family members had entered the remaining closet for shelter when the house was hit. The closet had save the persons life. I was amazed any human being could have survived such total devastation. Honeysuckle Drive and Country Club Boulevard was in complete shambles.

The area to the south of my brother's old home, had not been searched. Three officers and I maneuvered ourselves through the twisted debris and began our search. All the injured people had already been removed and transported to the hospital, according to the neighbors. On the way out of what was left of one home I noticed the east hallway had a strange tint to the paint. After a closer examination, I found countless numbers of fescue grass and clover leafs embedded in the paint and plaster. A particular clover leaf caught my eye. I tried to remove it; however, it had been slammed into the dry wall with such force I could not remove it. The fescue grass was in the same condition. The winds which caused the pieces of grass to fuse with the dry wall must have been incredible. Outside the front entrance door, we found a two-by-four inch pine stud slammed into the ground by the tornadic winds. About a foot of the board remained above the ground at an approximate forty-five degree angle. I could not resist the urge to pull the board from the ground to see exactly how far it had been pounded into the earth. It took four of our search team members and I to pull the board—which was nearly five feet long—from the ground. Some four feet of the stud had been slammed into the ground by the terrible wind. To this day I still find it hard to understand how that board could have been pushed that far into the ground by the winds of the tornado. We continued the search of the other damaged homes in the Country Club Edition. God had smiled upon them that day. There were no fatalities, however a few residents had suffered some fairly serious injuries.

Finally our sergeant told us we had to move on to the north central part of town. We were directed to the area of Hubbard Elementary School, on north Osage Ave. While en route, we saw a Red Cross and Salvation Army relief site had already been established. We stopped for a quick drink of cold water and a cup of hot soup. It was comforting knowing the Red Cross and Salvation Army had responded so quickly and were in full service. After the short break we were on our way to the redeployment site. We arrived at our destination near Osage Ave. and Johnson Street, approximately three statute miles from Southwest Village. The tornado had not lost any strength at that point. Some of the homes were completely destroyed and many were heavily damaged. The site mirrored what we had already witnessed in the other two areas. We searched until after dark. Most people's injuries were moderate; almost everyone had some cuts and bruises.

Our team found an elderly woman in a heavily damaged three–room house. A huge tree had penetrated the roof and come to rest upon the house. When we pushed our way inside I was shocked to see the woman rocking quietly in her rocking chair. She had suffered moderate lacerations and abrasions from the flying debris. Later we discovered she had refused to leave her home when her neighbors told her a tornado was coming. After some strong coaxing from us and her neighbors, she finally agreed to go to the hospital for treatment. We had uncovered only a few other persons in this area of our city.

Amazingly there were no fatalities. This fact puzzled most of us who were involved in the search and rescue operations. Sedalia was lucky the early warning had been issued by our local authorities. Lives were definitely saved.

The Missouri State Highway Patrol had sent dozens of troopers in answer to our requests aid for. And more were on the way. They were deployed all along the path to enhance security and thwart looting. I talked with many of the troopers as they arrived. A large number had never seen tornado damage before or if they had, not on such a scale as this.

The commanders of the State Patrol were assigned to the Command Post which was established in the basement of the Police Department. Commanders from the Missouri Army National Guard and Whiteman Air Force Base had also joined the Command Post. The Missouri Army National Guard had mobilized and was now on scene. At the time, I was a member of the Missouri Army National Guard and my unit was activated to help. The Joint Command Post made a decision to allow me to perform my duty as a police officer instead of a guardsman. I would assist as a liaison officer to the Guard while performing my duty as a police officer.

The sun had set and we were ordered to rally at the Police Department to regroup and redeployment as security teams. Each Sedalia Police Officer was assigned four Missouri Army National Guardsmen. We were very glad to have the National Guard augment our night patrols. Looting would soon be a problem and there is safety in numbers. Our clothes and uniforms were so soiled we could hardly stand each other. One by one we were relieved to clean up and return for duty. It really felt good to be clean again. I was glad to get into my police uniform instead of my street clothes. I met the four guardsmen who were assigned to me. They were armed with four foot wooden batons and helmets. I knew all four of them and they were good men. That was the good luck. The bad luck was the jeep they gave me to use for patrol had holes in the canvas top. It was raining again which made the roof leak terribly and it was raining rather hard. My duty raincoat helped keep me dry for a while but, by the time the sun came up I was soaked and cold. During the night we received two reports of looting in two different locations. The looters, or would—be looters were not expecting augmented police patrols. Four police officers arrived at the scene, with a total of sixteen baton toting Guardsmen behind them. It did not take but a second for the thieves to drop what they had and turn tail and run away. I am sure the word got out we were not going to tolerate any looting. We only had a limited number of looting events over the next two to three days.

The patrols ran all night and into the morning hours. Security perimeters were established in the most heavily damaged areas of town. We worked the perimeters during the day and patrols during the night. Finally after three days most of us were relieved from duty. I remember going home and taking a much needed shower. When I tried to remove my shoes I found one of my feet was so swollen I could not get the shoe off. Then I remembered the nail which had penetrated my foot in the Southwest Village subdivision. My foot and ankle were discolored and infected. My wife told me to get some sleep and she would order antibiotics from our doctor. She did not have to tell me twice. I closed my eyes and did not open them for about twenty hours. When I awoke I remember reflecting back on the entire ordeal. I was proud I had made it through my first major disaster as a supervisor. My command was not perfect, but it was adequate. The incredible thunderstorm which spawned the huge tornado eventually left our city and continued on its way. Even though the tornado dissipated, the powerful strong storm updrafts remain. Small parcels which are lifted up into a thunderstorm remain aloft until the updraft reduces or is carried out of the thunderstorm by winds aloft. There were many reports of Sedalia memorabilia finding its way to other towns around Missouri.

Articles from the *Sedalia Democrat Newspaper* amazed many of their readers when the following article were printed on May 9, 1977. The article was entitled "Computer card here found near Moberly." The article reads, Although 80 miles by today's standards is not too far, a wind-driven computer card traveling that distance is rather unusual.

Mrs. Raymond Flowers, who lives about 15 miles northeast of Moberly, Mo., near Duncan's Bridge, found such a computer card in her yard Wednesday afternoon, about 30 minutes after a tornado struck Sedalia.

The car, bearing the name of Sedalia optician Bernard M. Stanfield, was found by Mrs. Flowers following a storm with high winds and heavy rain. That storm was the same one that spawned the Sedalia tornado.

The card was $2.60 computer-printed bill from the Sedalia Country Club and was dated Dec. 6, 1972.

Stanfield said the tornado ripped the roof from his home, located at 1634 Honeysuckle in the Country Club addition. Old papers and receipts were stored in the attic, Stanfield said, adding that his home was demolished.

Although he had heard of two similar "finds" of his old documents, Stanfield noted both of those were in Sedalia. "The Sedalia Democrat ran another article on June 3, 1997; There is a lot of Sedalia still spread out over the countryside as a result of the May 4 tornado. But some of it is finding its way home. When the Don Braden house at 2505 Plaza was wiped out by the storm, one of the things lost was a large picture of their daughter, Carrie Lynn Griggs, then 2 years old.

On May 7, Ann Payne found the picture in a cornfield on her farm near Nelson Mo. Working only from the last name, Mrs. Payne was able to trace the picture to its owner. It survived the storm and the trip with only minor damage.

Sedalia has also been on the receiving end as well. Mrs. Jim Giokaris, 1123 West Seventh, found two photos in her yard after the tornado. One is a class shot of possibly sixth or seventh graders of several years back, and the other a color shot of a man in a chair with two children. The articles above furnish us an idea of the awesome forces which form and sustain a tornado. Inflow winds and updrafts play a major role in the strength of a tornado and its duration.

A friend of mine was a custodian at Mark Twain Elementary School. We were talking about the destructive winds of a tornado and of the odd things they can do. He quickly pointed out he saw a wooden plank pushed through a concrete ceiling at the school. Later an article in our local paper was printed showing the huge wooden plank which had been shoved through the concrete as my friend has said. The large plank had been driven into the concrete ceiling of a classroom.

The list of unique and bizarre incidents caused by tornados could go on for ever. The point I am trying to make is a simple one. The power generated by the rotating winds of a tornado can be deadly and dangerous. It is not a phenomenon to be taken lightly nor should tornados be chased by people who are not trained to do so. Tornados can hurl cars hundreds of feet, destroy a sturdy building, carry objects for eighty miles, and drive wood through concrete. If tornados can do all of this. . . think what it could do to you.

After recuperating from the ordeal, some of our local businesses desperately needed armed security for their buildings. It is not uncommon to see a store perfectly preserved on one side of the building with one entire wall missing, after a tornado strike. This was the case for one of our local department stores. The owner of the business knew me personally and inquired if I would consider guarding his valuables during the night time hours, until he could have it repaired. The money was good so I took the opportunity to work the security job.

The off duty employment began after my shift was over at 11:00 p.m. The owner of the business watched over things until I arrived. This went on for about a week. Even though I was glad to have the extra money, the hours were tough and long.

I remember one night in particular when I caught a looter, before he could strike. It was about 3:00 in the morning. I had been on the job for about four hours. The entire rear wall of the business was entirely open, so I stationed myself directly in the middle of the crippled building. Inside the business, much of the carpeting was wet and covered with debris. There were thousands of dollars worth of goods exposed. Television sets, jewelry, stereo units, and electrical merchandise were but a few of the items I was to guard.

It was very cloudy that evening, with intermittent thunderstorms smashing through our town. I remember one such thunderstorm which hit around midnight. I heard the thunder rumbling in the southwest. Lightning flashes began at a rate of three or four per minute. As the storm grew closer it intensified rapidly. Lightning strikes increases in numbers at such a rate it was nearly impossible to count them.

The storm struck with a wild fury. The already structurally compromised building was creaking and leaking terribly. Suddenly a west wind increased to around fifty to fifty-five miles per hour. I was standing in the middle of the store at this time in an attempt to stay dry and get away from the angry lightning strikes. The entire back section of the roof began to shake violently. Being a little gun-shy of falling timbers from the rescue attempt in Southwest Village, I found myself crawling under a large display case for shelter.

After two or three minutes of the strong winds the back section of the store's roof came crashing down. Debris, water, and insulation flew everywhere. After I determined I was still in one piece I left my safe place to investigate. The back of the store was a total loss. Thousands of dollars worth of electrical equipment and other valuable items were smashed. The rest of the merchandise was hopelessly rain–soaked. I wondered if the severe weather would ever end and what else could possibly go wrong.

After the series of thunderstorms moved out of the area the ground was saturated, causing a film of slick mud to coat about everything in site. I stepped to the rear of the building to scan the open field to the east of the building. I had moved people out of the field earlier. Some of then were just curious and not a threat to security; however, I am sure some were thinking about stealing from the open building.

As I was looking over the field, I noticed what appeared to be a pile of debris about one hundred feet east of the building. I did not remember the pile of debris being there before. As I watched, the pile of debris began to move toward me. I immediately drew my service revolver and took a defensive position, utilizing the cover and concealment that was available. I watched the looter crawl nearly ninety feet across the mud slick ground. When he was about ten feet away, I saw a large burlap bag in his right hand. I remained in my cover position and waited for the looter to approach me. As the now mud covered looter stood up, about five feet away, I stood up and shouted, "POLICE-DO NOT MOVE!"

The man threw his arms up and dropped the bag. He pleaded with me not to shoot him. I told the man to slowly turn around completely then to stop. I asked the looter if he had any weapons. He shook his head no. I then ordered the thief to put his hands against the wall. I quickly frisked him then read him his Miranda rights. He said he understood his rights. I told him to put his arms down and asked him his name and why he was crawling across the field with a burlap sack. He lowered his head and said that he wanted to pick up some "souvenirs" from the tornado. I asked him if the souvenirs he referred too could be radios, televisions, etc. He did not answer. I used my portable radio to call for a marked police unit. A car was immediately sent to assist me. The man was later found guilty of attempted theft.

Most of our citizens work together after a disaster strikes. But the few who can not resist the thought of getting something for nothing seems to get most the attention from our news media. The looter I arrested turned out to be an intelligent person and under normal circumstances, a law abiding citizen. Well, anyway, that's one that did not get away!

Because of my experience working the May 1977 tornado, I was much better prepared for the next one which occurred three years later in May of 1980. Alone and in a command position I learned exactly what the old saying meant by "the buck stops here!" Preparation for the next tornado is a never–ending job. Schools, churches, factories, medical care institutions continually tap the knowledge and expertise of local emergency management agencies across the nation.

Since then I have taught hundreds of severe weather and tornado safety classes. It feels good inside each time I give a presentation. You never know, one of the people you teach may survive "the next one" because of information they received. That one person may also be one less victim who has to be rescued. If just one life is saved, the entire effort is worthwhile.

Our local volunteer spotters received honorable mentions from the Missouri General Assembly, in Jefferson City, Missouri. One of the Civil Defense spotters, Reverend Greg Hibbard, was named "Sedalia Man of the Year." Greg received the award for his contribution during the tornado of 1977. He was credited with saving untold lives when he ordered the warning sirens to be activated before waiting for confirmation from ground spotters.

Chapter Five

Tornado Terror Strikes Again

MAY 12, 1980

Three years had passed since the May 1977 tornado struck our town. The community had recovered from the property damage and the frustrating reconstruction stage of the disaster. Almost all of the devastated homes and business had been reconstructed. A few empty lots remained as testimony to the terrible tornado which struck on "Black Wednesday," and several other solemn reminders remained as they had been left three years ago to remind us of the awesome power of the twister. But many survivors felt a bone chilling fear each time the clouds gathered and thunder was heard in the distant sky. The fear of another tornado striking our town was most obviously noticed in the children. They did not have the ability to discern between a harmless spring thunder shower and thunderstorms which spawn killer tornados.

Many local psychologists donated their time and efforts to help the children of our city cope with their fears. It took time and considerable effort to accomplish their goal; however, the end result was worthwhile. Slowly but surely our children gradually put aside their fears of experiencing another tornado and came to understand the phenomenon and how to cope with it.

The Sedalia School District played large role in helping the children recover from their nightmare memories of the 1977 tornado. Tornado drills were commonplace and continue to this very day. The repeated drills reenforced and enhanced the chances of survival should a tornado threaten the schools. Interaction between teachers, emergency response personnel and students helped them understand they were not alone with their fears of the whirling giant. The mere act of getting the kids to talk about them appeared to ease their apprehension. This kind of interaction, basically group therapy, allowed for the eventual partial healing of our kids. But each of them, as well as many adults, still have a deep feeling of apprehension which will never completely disappear. Maybe people who live in and around "Tornado Alley" need this deep down fear. Maybe it is nature's way of helping them to survive another "Black Wednesday."

It was 1980 and I had been promoted to the rank of sergeant. The promotion had brought on many new responsibilities. The Sedalia Police Department was also expanding its responsibilities and services to our community. Due to my close affiliation with the Civil Defense Agency, our department decided to add a new unit, the Severe Storms Detachment. I was appointed by Sedalia Police Chief Philip Schnabel to command our newly formed unit. I was proud to command this unit; however, the fear of making a poor decision was a always in the back of my mind. Chief Schnabel was not only a perfectionist, he believed their was no such word as failure. I knew I had to do this right.

Our primary mission was to assist the Civil Defense Agency chase and report severe thunderstorms and tornados. But our main concern was protecting the City of Sedalia proper. The Civil Defense Agency was charged with the same mission; however, they had to cover all of Pettis County.

When the National Severe Storms Forecast Center issued a severe thunderstorm or tornado watch, we would deploy somewhere near the southwest city limits and concentrate our efforts in that quadrant of the county. We used multi-channel radios to communicate with Civil Defense Spotters, the County Sheriff's Department, and our police communications section. The Sedalia Police Department was, and still is, the warning point for Pettis County and Sedalia. The police communications section was linked to hundreds of federal, state, and local warning points by a system known as (NAWAS) The National Warning System. National Weather Service Offices were included in the circuit, thus providing immediate communications with them.

Besides myself, the other members of the team were, Sergeant Rene Dedrick, Officer Ed Bone, Officer John Rosebrock, and Officer Bill Chapman. We spent hundreds of hours waiting for incoming super cell thunderstorms to enter our area. The time we spent was good training and gave us time to communicate with other storm chasers in the local Civil Defense as well as neighboring counties. It is crucial to know personally who is giving you information, since your actions and decisions must be based on their reports. You must be able to trust their judgments in order to make your own. The better you know the spotters the better you can make judgments based on their information.

Before the days of Doppler Radars, instant radar plots from the Internet, and other systems, currently used for warning and detection of severe weather, the role of the surface observer was extremely critical. This meant hundreds of hours waiting for something to move in or develop within your area. As I said before, the surface observer is still important to the National Weather Service and always will be although some of the extreme pressure has lessened over the past few years.

Beginning in 1978, the (SSD) Severe Storms Detachment, had two years to prepare operations before dealing with the devastation of the May 12, 1980 tornado, time which was put to good use by the members of the team. Our interrelationship with the storm–chasing community had grown by leaps and bounds. I will tell you about some of our experiences during this period to give you an idea how we worked and sometimes played.

We had several local giants in the storm chasing community to use as role models and mentors. Most notable were the following storm chasers from our Civil Defense Agency: Kenneth Mickens, John Burford, Bill Watring, Greg Hibbard, and Bill Hill. These five men had chased and reported severe thunderstorms and tornados for many years and had gained the respect and admiration of our community and our SSD Unit. Ken Mickens and Bill Hill worked for the Missouri Pacific Railroad repair shop, located in Sedalia. Greg Hibbard was a minister in a local Lutheran Church, John Burford was an established plumber in Sedalia and Bill Watring was retired. From my perspective, these outstanding storm chasers provided me with much of the information and experience I needed to further my career in the field and I could not have been luckier to have such mentors.

I am reminded of a scores of severe weather events, some of which pushed the envelope of any storm chaser. Some very close calls with tornados and gut–wrenching ninety plus mile–per–hour straight line winds terrorized even the most seasoned veterans. Putting the danger aside we spent hundreds of hours just waiting for an event to take place. Sometimes not a single rain drop would fall. All we could do was watch the lightning skirt around Pettis County.

Here is what a typical day of storm watching in West-Central Missouri looks like. Usually, we would know the night before that a front or storm system was heading our way. The late night news and weather would provide a clue.

After the late night weather the phone would ring. Someone would be calling to give you an opinion on what would happen the next day. Of course, you would have to call someone else to give them your opinion. This would go on for hours.

The next day it all began again. We would stay in constant contact with each other figuring out who would be riding with whom later on during the late afternoon hours. Long before the Weather Service issued severe weather watches, we had a pretty good idea which way the storms would be approaching, where we could get the best view of the approaching storm, and a fairly good estimate of just how severe the storms would be. Formulating this kind of preliminary information was our spotter group's reason for existing and we loved it.

Spotters in West Central Missouri would always pay special attention to southeastern Kansas and northeastern Oklahoma weather conditions. Usually, early in the afternoon we would meet at the police department or the Civil Defense Office to listen to the NAWAS phone. This gave us a good excuse to have coffee together and "talk shop."

The friendships we developed would last us a lifetime. I can honestly say some of the most remarkable and most rememberable times of my life have been spent with my fellow storm chasers. They are a special breed of people. Most are dedicated to serving their communities and science.

Generally, the afternoon would drag on slowly. We knew the best chance of severe weather was in the mid- to late-afternoon hours and we could feel the tension mount as the skies slowly became overcast. The "Weather Channel" on our local cable system provided us new opportunities to view enhanced imagery which we had never had at our disposal before. Current radar imagery, weather satellites, and surface plots gave us an edge prior to the storm's arrival. We added the channel to our Emergency Operations Center to give our Civil Defense Director current information which could be relayed to the field spotters by radio.

As the reports of severe weather increased from Kansas or Olklahoma, the anticipation level would peak. Early spring tornado watches would be issued by the Weather Service far in advance of the approaching or developing storm systems. As a rule of thumb, the tornado watches would be issued between two and five o'clock in the afternoon. Some would last for six hours. We knew we would be included in the watch box area as the day progressed.

As soon as the National Weather Service Office issued a tornado or severe thunder storm watch, the Sedalia Police Department would call me to mobilize our Severe Storms Detachment Unit. We used a Dodge Maxivan to chase tornados. The van, previously an evidence collection unit, had been converted to suit the needs of our unit. Many of the shelves and drawers which had been installed were used to store maps, spotter locations, outdoor warning siren locations, and a wealth of other weather related chart and paraphernalia. The most useful part of the van was an outside platform built on top. Originally the platform had been used for a cam-corder which took overhead shots of a particular crime scene. Now we stood on it to view cloud formations and approaching fronts. Once we got the word . . . we were off. The spotter network was now officially activated, even though we had been out "un-officially" for hours.

In the late seventies our Civil Defense Agency changed from Citizen Band Radios to Business Band radios. The FM radios gave us a cleaner channel to operate on and a more secure environment. Our van was outfitted with a 100 watt transmitter receiver with two channels. One channel was for the Sedalia Police Department, the other was for the Civil Defense frequency.

It was a real sight to see this unit going down the road. It did not take long for the citizens to figure out that when our van left the station, severe weather would soon follow. As soon as the word got around, the spotter network sprang to life. Radio chatter increased, spotters would be deployed, and countless numbers of donated hours of service would be given to our community. Usually we would find a place for our wind detection devices and install them and look for a place for immediate shelter, just in case. This usually meant a ditch or a ravine.

Radios would be checked and the (EOC) Emergency Operations Center would plot our locations on a master board. The CD director must always keep track of who is where. Spotter locations are very important to the agency because the director may have to move a spotter away from an approaching tornado or change a spotter's location to assist in finding one. Another reason to keep close tally on spotter locations is for their personal safety. If a spotter had to leave the vehicle because a tornado was getting too close, we had to be able to quickly send help as soon as it was safe to do so.

As the cool front collided with the humid warm air mass to our southwest, we could see lightning on the far distant horizon. The tops of the approaching thunderstorms would climb into the thirty, forty, and fifty thousand foot range. The adjoining counties to our south, south west, and west are Benton, Henry, and Johnson Counties, respectively. Reports of funnel clouds, damaging high winds, and large hail from their areas helped us re-deploy our spotters to get a better look at the proper area of the storms as they approached us.

We would monitor multi-channel scanning receiver monitors, AM and FM radio stations, and up to three channel receiver-transmitter radios all going at the same time. A half dozen smaller towns which surrounded our community would also deploy their own spotters. It was not unusual for fifteen spotters to be exchanging information at one time. Needless to say, the noise level in a spotter's vehicle would cause an unexperienced person to pull out his or her hair. But, after a few years of experience you learned to discern between which information was pertinent and which was not.

As the storm approached spotters in the outlying areas would radio information to the EOC: wind speed, wind direction, the number of times lightning struck the ground, in one minute and heavy precipitation or hail reports. Using this information as a baseline, we would determine the severity of the storm as it crept closer. If the surface winds reached severe limits we would issue are own severe thunderstorm warning. If it decreased in intensity we would remain just in case the storm re-developed. Most of the more seasoned spotters would use hand-held wind speed indicators to determine the surface winds. The problem with this device was you had to roll down your window and point it in the direction the wind was blowing. As a result the inside of the spotter's vehicle would most always get soaked by the driving rain.

As the storm proceeded through our county we repositioned ourselves to get a better look at the backside of the storm, more specifically the southwestern corner of the storm, "the bear's cage." It was imperative to position our spotters strategically to ensure that no tornado slipped through unseen. To support the spotter watching the rear of the cell we would also place two more spotters around the main storm towers, one on the east side and one on the west side. This type of deployment would prevent our missing a tornado which might be embedded in a rain shaft. Remember, you cannot see an approaching tornado from the front of the thunderstorm, it is behind the heavy rain shaft. To my knowledge, we have missed only one tornado as of this date. That particular tornado developed on the extreme northern portion of Pettis County, a sparely populated area with few spotters.

After the first storm left our area we checked on each other to make sure all was well. This meant it was time for a coke or a cup of coffee together, if time permitted. I can remember many war stories over a cup of coffee with John Burford and Kenny Mickens. Kenny would also include numerous stories about his close friend, Bill Hill. Bill and Kenny worked together for many years at the Missouri Pacific Railroad Shops in our community. Kenny always referred to Bill as "Ole Fats," a name which Bill learned to live with after many years. Bill was a storm spotter as well. The Weather Service Office would keep us updated on newly developed thunderstorms and approximately how long it would be before it entered our jurisdiction. Without local radar support we would be forced to sit there for hours and upon occasion, days.

Inside our Police Department Maxi-Van offered our Severe Storms Detachment Team easy access to cloud formation charts, Outdoor Warning Siren Location Charts, and an array of electronic gizmos that enhanced our ability to hear incoming reports of severe weather from other counties and cities. The van was very stable in high winds and its inside setup allowed for quick access to dozens of storage bins which contained first-aid equipment and other emergency response equipment. We also had our own generator which could generate enough power for our portable outside quartz-halogen light set.

I have many a fond memory of days and nights huddled inside our van waiting for "the big one." Usually it was warm and muggy. Our jump suits were lightweight but still hot. Our van was not air conditioned. Finding a good spot to watch storms from the shade was not always easy. More than likely you would find us inside the van playing rummy or hearts in between storm cells. Sergeant Dedrick and Officer Chapman always beat me in cards. I knew they were cheating but I could not tell how. I still do not know. Piles of potato chip wrappers, sandwiches, and empty coke cans gave us a rough idea of just how long we had been out there. The longest time I remember being out on storm watch was thirty-six hours, in the mid 1980's. A series of storms were "training" through our area one after another. Each had to be carefully observed.

Late spring of 1980 was an active year for severe storms in and around the central Missouri area. We survived many severe thunderstorm and tornado watches, some of which were near misses from rotating funnel clouds and/or tornados.

Monday, May 12, 1980.

I did not know what terrors would unfold that day when a monster F4 tornado erased the northwestern corner of our city.

Sunday evening we viewed the weather maps for the next day. A low pressure system was approaching from the west. A large area of warm moisture laden air was in place over Central Missouri. A cool front was eastbound from the Rocky Mountains bringing cool dry air the perfect mix to spawn tornados within super cell thunderstorms.

It was part of my job as supervisor of the Severe Storms Detachment to know when the risk of severe weather was present and plan accordingly. I took my job very seriously and I still do.

Monday morning brought warm balmy temperatures to our community. By any standards it was a beautiful morning. As the day progressed, southwest winds increased with gusts to thirty miles per hour. By noon temperatures had soared to the mid eighties. The National Weather Service Office in Columbia, Missouri issued a severe weather advisory for west-central and central Missouri for the mid to late afternoon hours. Thunderstorms were beginning to break out in advance of the approaching cool front in western and southern Missouri. The Police Department Communications Officer called me at 1401 hours. She had been monitoring the NAWAS line and learned the thunderstorms to our west and southwest were approaching severe limits.

I arrived at the police department ten minutes later. Our point to point radio frequency was going wild. The thunderstorms were big and were expected to get a whole lot bigger.

The National Severe Storms Forecast Center, in Kansas City, Missouri, issued a tornado watch for our area. The tornado watch was number 102 and was valid from 1530 to 2300 hours. I still have the original tornado watch and the associated articles and media clippings. The watch read as follows:

ATTN: OFFICERS 1532 MAY 12 DE NATNL WX SVC BULLETIN: IMMEDIATE BROADCAST REQUESTED TORNADO WATCH NUMBER 102 NATIONAL WEATHER SERVICE KANSAS CITY MO THE NATIONAL SEVERE STORMS FORECAST CENTER HAS ISSUED A TORNADO WATCH FOR

CENTRAL AND WEST CENTRAL MISSOURI

SMALL PART OF NORTHEAST KANSAS

FROM 330 PM CDT UNTIL 9 PM CDT THIS MONDAY AFTERNOON AND EVENING TORNADOS. . . LARGE HAIL. . . . AND DAMAGING THUNDERSTORM WINDS ARE POSSIBLE IN THESE AREAS.

THE TORNADO WATCH AREA IS ALONG AND 70 STATUTE MILES EITHER SIDE OF ALINE FROM 20 MILES WEST OF KANSAS CITY MISSOURI TO 30 MILES NORTH NORTHEAST OF VICHY MISSOURI

REMEMBER. . .A TORNADO WATCH MEANS CONDITIONS ARE FAVORABLE FOR TORNADOS AND SEVERE THUNDERSTORMS IN AND CLOSE TO THE WATCH AREA

I listened to the NAWAS line for the most current reports of severe weather. Many of the towns to the west of our area were reporting severe thunderstorms and damage reports. At 1401 hours I heard the Columbus Missouri Police Department report a tornado touchdown. The tornado was moving east-northeast at forty miles per hour. I went to discuss the situation with Civil Defense Director, Jim Snavely, at the Emergency Operations Center which was located deep in the basement of the court house. Jim and I plotted the tornado watch boundaries on a plot map. From the information we had available we believed the threat potential was very high for tornadic activity. Jim said he was going to activate the Civil Defense spotters and place them earlier than normal. I agreed and told him I would activate our team as well.

I called Officer John Rosebrock at his home and told him about the tornado watch. I also told him we already had a quite remarkable development to our west. John came right down. After he and I checked out our van we decided to deploy to the southwest portion of the city near the city limits. The air was very muggy and the stiff southwest wind was welcomed. Before we left I called my mother to alert her to the tornado risk. She would contact the rest of the family.

Soon the Civil Defense Spotter Network began to come alive. The Operations Commander for the Civil Defense Agency was Kenny Mickens. When Kenny came up on the air we gave him our position. Kenny placed ten spotters and put others on stand by, should the watch be extended late into the night. John and I felt very uneasy that day. We knew the stiff southwest wind added shear to the middle layer where the thunderstorms would be developing, a key ingredient for tornados to develop. We placed our wind direction indicator and waited.

Sedalia Police Officers Ed Bone and Manly White came to our location. They were on routine patrol and wanted to check the weather situation after they received the tornado watch information. Officer Bone told me he had never seen a tornado and was really anxious to see one. I told Ed I'd let him know if and when we spotted a tornado. His partner Officer White had seen them before and was not too interested in our conversation.

We waited with the other spotters scanning various radio frequencies in an attempt to get a heads up on locations of area thunderstorms. It appeared most of the action would remain to our west for quite some time. At approximately 1625 hours we were observing a large thunderstorm developing approximately fifteen miles west southwest of Sedalia and growing rapidly. We could

see the approaching rain shaft which was bent at 45 degree angle from the strong southernly winds. A lightning
count of fifteen per minute was consistently being reported by spotters to our south and west. The National
Weather Service Office in Columbia, Missouri issued a
severe thunderstorm warning for Pettis and Saline Counties at 1630 hours. Our awareness level jumped up very
quickly. We knew a tornado could form instantly in these
kinds of conditions.

At 1700 hours we received information from our
Civil Defense Emergency Operations Center. The Missouri State Highway Patrol had confirmed a report of a
tornado on the ground just east of Whiteman Air Force
Base about fifteen miles to our west southwest. The National Weather Service Office at Columbia Missouri also
indicated a tornado on their radar. The tornado was moving east northeast at forty miles per hour.

John and I knew what that meant. We prepared to
move out and relocate to the Heritage Village Trailer Park
just a few block to our east. Hundreds of mobile homes
were in danger. If a tornado warning was issued by the
Weather Service, we would use our siren and public address system to warn the occupants of the mobile home
park. No public shelter was located within the park itself.
Seconds seemed like hours before we heard anything
from our EOC. John and I were getting a little nervous.
The thunder was getting closer and much louder.

Suddenly the Civil Defense Director came on the air.
His voice cracking somewhat, he gave the following message: A tornado warning had issued for the city of Sedalia
and Pettis County, Missouri. Immediately thereafter the
outdoor warning sirens began to blast. As the sirens
wailed John and I advised the police department we
would be warning Heritage Village Mobile Home Park.
We instinctively turned on the local AM and FM radio

stations to see if they had received the information. They had and were switching to emergency operations.

I told John to drive into the mobile home park. He activated the emergency lights on the van and used the manual siren to get the occupants' attention. As I announced the grave information over the PA system in between John's siren blasts, people began running all over the place, getting their family and friends into their cars to seek shelter. On our last trip through the park John and I noticed five adults had put folding chaise lounge chairs on the western end of the trailer park. We advised them to leave. They said they were staying and were going to watch the tornado. They also had a small infant with them. They were drinking beer and were obviously intoxicated. I told them they could stay but I was going to take custody of the child and report them to the Division of Family Service. I also told them they would most likely lose their child hoping to convince them to go. Finally the mother of the child decided to leave and take the child to safety. The others stayed.

We left the trailer park and proceeded to a local shopping center to give warning, all the while were watching the southwestern horizon. We knew from reports of other spotters the tornado was still three miles out. Traffic was completely jammed on the major routes. It was also rush hour in our town. We decided to make one more trip through the trailer court. The five intoxicated people were gone. Maybe the intense thunder and lightning had forced them out. We will never know.

The rain was beginning to get heavier and we decided it was time to seek shelter ourselves. According to the other spotters on the net the tornado was approaching our west city limit. We had pre-selected our shelter site earlier, the basement of a local motel, Ramada Inn, on the west city limits. As we neared the motel we saw people running all over the Sunset Village Trailer Park. There was no order or special direction they were running; they were just in a panic. But now it was too late. There was nothing we could do to help them. We arrived at the Ramada Inn as the rain turned to hail. It was apparent we were in the line of this now full–blown tornado. Behind the heavy hail would be the violently rotating vortex. We knew we had only a few minutes before we were toast, but wo had time to seek the protection of the motel's basement. We parked our van and took a quick look towards the approaching tornado. The hail was now the size of golf balls and coming down very hard.

We exited the van and began to run across the parking lot to the east door of the motel. It is hard to believe but, the very instant we exited the van, the hail grew to the size of softballs or even somewhat bigger. The hail stones had protruding spikes on them and they were now beginning to come at us from the south, horizontally with the pavement. The tornado was just behind the hail shaft, no more than two or three blocks away. We could hear the "hissing" sound of the wind surrounding the vortex. I pulled at the door to the motel but it was locked. Let me make something very clear. During the entire time we were warning the public, neither of us were what you would call frightened. NOW WE WERE FRIGHTENED.

What little light that had made it through eleven miles of clouds above was now gone. It was dark as night. John and I could hear the deafening roar of the tornado now just a few hundred yards away. We could see small pieces of debris to the north of the vortex but we still could not see the tornado. Our adrenalin glands were now working overtime. Then John noticed the red lights on the van were running. For some weird reason, he decided to run to the van and shut off the lights. He was dodging hail balls and a terrific straight line wind. I watched with amazement as he darted to the van, shut off the lights, locked the door, then sprinted back to the locked door where I was standing. I looked at him but I could not say anything. We were in big time trouble and nowhere to go.

John yelled at the top of his lungs, "WE HAVE TO GET INSIDE!" I could not disagree with him so I made a command decision. I told John to step back. I unholstered my service revolver and aimed it at the door lock. We were going to get in. . . we had no choice. The tornado was closing in fast and it was becoming more difficult to breath. At that moment the manager of the motel walked in front of the glass door. He was going to look outside to see where the tornado was; instead he was looking down the business end of my service revolver. The manager threw up his hands not knowing exactly what I was doing. In retrospect, I do not blame him.

I put my gun away immediately. The manager opened the door and let us in, though he was still quite confused. I asked him if all of his guests were in the basement. He replied, "I think so." We ran to where we though the basement entrance was located. Instead of finding the guests in the basement, they were all standing near the west door on the first floor. If the tornado remained on course they, along with us, would most certainly be killed.

John and I quickly ordered the guests, they numbered around thirty, to the basement. They did as we ordered. We were now certain we had only seconds to get to shelter ourselves. We started to go to the basement with the other guests when we were faced with a most dangerous dilemma. In their hurried evacuation of the upper floors. The man was on crutches and was panic stricken.

We did not have to discuss our plan. John and I ran to the older gentleman without talking to each other. We knew the tornado must be very near the motel by now.

But we were out of time and we were on the first floor of the motel and not in the basement. To compound our situation even more the elderly man was standing near the west glass entrance door. John and I looked see outside. It was now pitch black and we could see the double glass doors moving in and out from the approaching tornado.

Then without warning, the lights inside the motel went out. We were sunk. The only thing we could do was to protect the old man and somehow ourselves the best to our ability, considering the circumstances. I told John to place the man on the floor face down. Then we both lay on top of him with our faces down. The very second we covered the old man both of the glass doors were pulled open by the rotation of the tornado. It was just about one hundred yards to our west. We could see all sorts of debris being whirled around the vortex. Grass and tree limbs were flying by at an incredible rate of speed. The old man began to cry. We told him we were going to be alright, although we were not exactly sure this was true. We could feel our very breath being pulled from our lungs. It was very hard to breath now and the roar of the winds were like that of an angry devil. We also heard the huge tornado's distinctive hissing sound.

It was all over within a few seconds. But they were the longest seconds of our lives to this very day. It became very still and very quiet. We knew we had been spared a direct hit. After a short prayer of thanks we helped the old man to his feet. He was not injured and had stopped crying. With a bowed head he thanked us. We handed him his crutches then exited the west door which was only a few feet away.

Once outside the motel John and I instinctively looked to the west and the north of where we were standing. What we saw would humble a saint. The Highway 50

Drive In Theater was gone. Nothing remained. We looked north of where the Drive In used to be to see what was left of the Sunset Village Mobile Home Park. Remember, just minutes before the tornado struck we had seen scores of people running everywhere. We were both speechless. Almost all the Mobile Home Park had been flattened like a pancake. We did not see anyone moving about. As we looked northeast we saw the giant tornado churning its way east-northeast.

The next target on the tornado's hit list was the Kelsy-Hayes Manufacturing Plant. We stared in disbelief as the the tornado held its course toward the giant factory. When it hit it was like something from a science fiction movie. The west walls of the factory collapsed and the rest of the huge steel sided building exploded as if an enormous bomb had been detonated. After watching this display of natural power we could hardly move, but we had to report what we had seen and get over to the effect area. We ran the best as we could with shaky legs to our police van, relieved to see it was still there. The dents in the body left by the softball-sized hail were obvious but it was still operational.

We tried to get onto the radio with our emergency traffic. It was near impossible. Every officer in the city was trying to give spot locations of the tornado or report damages or injuries. I decided to go to the Sunset Village Mobile Home Park and establish a Command Post. From the west end of the trailer park to the east end of the Kelsy-Hayes Factory was about a half mile, a half mile of total devastation. We knew there must be serious injuries and most likely many deaths.

En route to the trailer park we finally got on the air. We gave the dispatcher the information we had and told her we were going to establish a Forward Command Post near the devastated area and that we needed as many officers as we could get. We also asked for mutual aid assistance from area jurisdictions; we needed fire fighting equipment, ambulances, and additional law enforcement support. The dispatcher confirmed our request with a 10-4. She also said it would some time before we could get assistance. Bccn thoro . . . done that! We understood the situation. I told John to get on the Civil Defense Radio and ask for assistance from people on our volunteer force who were not actively chasing the tornado.

John Burford, from the Civil Defense, was one of the first volunteers to arrive. John went into the trailer court to do a cursory damage assessment, meanwhile John and I began to set up shop. The very first thing we had to do was to select a site which would be accessible, yet not too far from the area so we could observe what was actually going on. Later when more support arrived we could back off, but not now. It was all up to us for the time being.

We selected a site about half way between what was left of the Sunset Village Mobile Home Park and the now destroyed Kelsy-Hayes Manufacturing Factory and we sealed off the Command Post area with yellow tape. Radio contact was rechecked. John Burford, who was now deep within the rubble of the trailer park, said he had injuries and needed medical assistance. We relayed his report to the police department. Ambulance units were directed to the command post. We used a large parking lot near by to stage emergency responders and their equipment.

The first units began to arrive. All of our Pettis County Ambulance Units were sent our way. Fire Department support was also requested by our Command Post. We believed people might be trapped within the large factory and underneath debris in the trailer court. We had been on scene for a half an hour when the police dispatcher called and said the Mayor had requested federal assistance from Whiteman Air Force Base, twenty miles to our west. They were sending ambulances, security police, and rescue fire equipment to the command post. John and I were amazed at the way area jurisdictions offered assistance to our community. As additional police officers arrived at the scene we began to organize a search party which would be sent inside the Kelsy-Hayes Plant and the huge area of destroyed mobile homes at Sunset Village.

The tornado had left our county but was still moving east northeast at forty miles per hour. We were pleasantly surprised to hear most of the damage was limited to the northwest corner of the city. Some houses and smaller business had suffered damages. Another factory on State Fair Boulevard had lost the entire building had been next to the main factory. That building was about two blocks long and a block wide. Miraculously the employees suffered only minor injuries.

The sun began to shine on the western part of town. The total distruction of sixty mobile homes and an entire industrial complex had taken less than one minute. It seemed ironic that the sun could shine so brightly and the sky could be so clear after such a catastrophe. It is mind boggling.

We were told that the Emergency Room at Bothwell Regional Health Center was receiving many patients, most of whom had been taken to the hospital by friends and loved ones. We were into the operation about an hour when we received a radio call from John Burford. It was the call we had been fearing. John had located a group of people who were trying to raise a large portion of a mobile home frame. Apparently, their friend had been inside when the tornado struck. John was requesting a crane to assist in the rescue. Fire fighters from the city and county fire department were now on the scene. I notified the police department. They said they would contact a heavy equipment company for help.

A privately—owned bulldozer and operator was sent to the scene. It did not take long for the crew to get there, no more than thirty minutes from the time the call was placed by the police dispatcher. After carefully planning their strategy the bulldozer operator went to work. Tediously and slowly the debris was removed. Fire Department personnel sifted through the debris but could not find the victim. The worried friends and family of the victim feared the worst; however, the police department dispatcher soon called to tell me the victim had somehow lived through the tornado and had been taken to the hospital by civilian rescuer. John Burford and the other rescuers were certainly pleased to hear the victim was safe and not buried under tons of debris.

The total devestation of the trailer park made organized search and rescue efforts difficult to implement. We could not determine where the roads began and ended. Debris was piled on top of debris. Only the skeletal remains of what used to be mobile homes remained and even those were scattered blocks away from where they should have been. We were forced to use a grid search pattern. Groups of rescuers were given geographical blocks instead of organized blocks to search. We had to be sure that each search area overlapped the adjacent search areas to avoid skipping over rubble which might contain an injured person or dead body.

Once the search parties were organized and deployed I established a similar search party to enter the Kelsy-Hayes factory. The team was comprised of two Sedalia firemen, Officer Rosebrock and myself, and an Emergency Medical Technician from one of our local ambulance companies. We entered the factory from what was left of the main entrance on the south side of the structure. Before we entered we yelled as loudly as we could so any surviors could hear us and respond. And once inside the factory we stopped every 50 feet to listen for surviors. answers.

The devastation was enormous. The twisted steel I-beam girders looked like pretzels or pieces of spagettie. Electrical wires had been ropped from their conduit pipes and were arcing all around.

We had information that the workers who were in the plant at the time of the tornado touchdown were to use the backroom for a tornado shelter. But we were still a long way from the backroom when about halfway through the search we smelled natural gas hissing and leaking from a rupture line just ahead. We moved slowly around the debris, afraid we would cause the metal to shift and cause a spark which would ignite the natural gas.

We inched our way to the rear of the plant coming closer to the break room with every step. The twisted metal was far beyond anything I had ever seen before. Huge I-beams were actually bent double to the ground then back again as if they were a huge pretzels. Large industrial machinery lay broken and turned over by the impacting winds from the tornado.

We finally arrived at our destination. But much to our surprise found no survivors left in the break room. They had apparently found a way out of the broken building on their own. We left the same way we had entered feeling somewhat disappointed. Later we learned there had been many injuries inside the break room but none of them were serious. The pre-planned tornado sheltering plan had done its job.

We rejoined our Forward Command Post which was now being operated by police dispatcher Carolyn Dalton and other officers which arrived to assist. We had been into the disaster just a few hours but it felt like two days.

Ambulances and fire fighting equipment streamed into the Command Post. There must have been fifty ambulances lined up at one time. I actually had to turn some of them back. I can honestly say that mid-Missourians are great people. We may fight among are selves but during emergencies we always come through for each other.

I met with the Civil Defense Director, Jim Snavely, to make a plan of action as night was only some three hours away. We both knew the residents of the mobile home park would soon be returning to try to salvage anything they could from their destroyed homes. We were smpathetic but we could not let the now homeless people into the restricted area until we could took care of live power lines and ruptured gas lines. And knowing the possibility of the proposition of getting something for nothing sometimes makes people do things they normally would not do, we feared thieves and looters would soon be making their presence known once they had the cover of darknes.

Our communications officer told us Missouri Army National Guardsmen from our local unit would be coming in about an hour. We decided to use these guardsmen for perimeter sentries. I made a quick plan to determine the spacing and assignment numbers for each post.

I had plenty of officers and firemen at our area so I sent word back to police headquarters they could reassign some of the people who had been assigned to me. Areas north and east of our position had been hit hard as well. We sent ten or so officers to be reassigned to the other area commands which would need security as well. All telephones lines in the area were down and would not be repaired for quite some time. Electricity was near non-existent. I asked the fire department to send us emergency portable lights and a generator. This would help us secure the area when the sun went down and darkness set in.

Officer Ed Bone and his partner Manly White arrived at the Command Post. Their squad car looked as if it had been in a combat zone. Ed approached the Command Post with a bewildered look on his face and a sheepish grin. I knew something had happened but exactly what I did not know. Ed began the conversation with a question. He asked me if I remember our earlier conversation before the tornado had hit. I told him I remembered and I asked him if he had seen the twister. Ed grinned and answered, " We saw it alright, it was on top of us and we did not know it." He went on to tell me when the tornado warning was issued they listened to Officer Rosebrock and me describe where the tornado was and in what direction it was going. Ed, wanting to see a tornado, talked Officer White into parking their patrol car northeast of where the tornado had already been reported on the ground. Ed exited the patrol car, much to Officer White's dismay and stood in the roadway waiting for the spectacle to appear.

Ed said he could hear the deafening roar and the hissing of the high winds around the vortex, but he could not see the tornado. Ed was quite frustrated being this close but not seeing the monster twister. Suddenly, Ed said the super large hail started falling striking him numerous times. He looked up and saw what he had come to see.

The gray colored tornado was around two hundred yards wide and was scattering debris everywhere. The tornado was moving quicker than he anticipated. So Ed clung to the base of a tree as the tornado passed overhead. He said, "It lifted me up and slammed me back to the ground." He added, the only way the tornado was going to take him was if the tree went too. After it passed over him he watched the tornado hit two houses just north of his location. He and Officer White checked out the residents of the homes after it was safe to do so. They had survived the tornado by going to their basement for shelter. Fortunately for both Ed and his partner, who had remained in the car, the tornado had lifted just enough to save their lives. Badly hit, Ed revealed the bruises to his back where the softball sized hail had struck him while he hung onto the base of the tree.

After the tornado had passed both officers thanked God they were still alive. Ed had left the squad car door open on his side of the car. And when he got back to the car he was amazed to see massive tree limb impaled from his side of the car all the way into where Officer White was sitting. After they removed the limb they noticed a small lizard sitting on the dash of their patrol car. Apparently the lizard had been sitting on the limb when it was slung into the open car door.

Officer Bone told me the tornado he had seen was awesome, but he had seen enough. I agreed with him and we both had a good laugh. Ed and Manly returned to their patrol duties somewhat more educated in the art of tornado watching.

I heard a helicopter overhead and it appear to be circling in what I thought was an attempt to land. I first believed it to be a military helicopter but, after a second look it was obvious it was a news media helicopter one of several I had seen. There was no place close which did not have scattered debris from one end to the other. If a helicopter landed in one of these areas it could be disastrous. I had our communications officer send for our street department. I had them come to our Command Post and quickly clear an area which could be used for an emergency Landing Zone (LZ). The Street Department employees did an excellent job and just in time. The helicopter pilot must have understood the situation and waited until it was safe to land his aircraft. Eventually eight aircraft carrying television reporters and military support personnel shared this make-shift landing zone.

We were beginning to feel the effects of not eating for some while. You need to replace the energy you expend and we were in desperate need of sanitary drinking water as well. As the two agencies have done dozens of times before, the American Red Cross and the Salvation Army came through for us. Their field food units arrived and reported to the Command Post. We set up a schedule so the deployed police officers and firemen had time to eat a quick sandwich and drink some ice cold water. I cannot say enough about these two fine organizations. In an uncertain and often times hostile environment it is most comforting to rescue workers and victims alike knowing they will be there when the entire world around them seems to be falling apart.

Advanced elements of the local National Guard Unit arrived at the Command Post and coordinated assignments and tasks. The commander of the troops offered all the assistance he had and would get more if we needed it. He agreed to the plan Jim and I had devised and assigned two sergeants to the Command Post as liaison NCO's. Once the perimeter was secured by guardsmen. I recalled the assigned police and fire officials who had been posted early on. Sedalia Police Officers were assigned to emergency twelve hour shifts until the situation moderated. Sedalia and Pettis County Firemen returned to their companies for follow up duties. The Missouri State Highway Patrol maintained traffic control in and around the disaster area which kept hundreds of sight seekers from clogging our emergency exits and entrances.

Our joint command was not only working, but working well. Communications channels were assigned to groups. As long as you can communicate you can remain in control. In situations involving mass destruction and long distances communication is absolutely essential.

As the sun began to set we finally had time to eat something and make plans for the hundreds of residents we knew would be returning to the area the next day hoping to find something which could be salvaged. Our plan called for the use of colored identification cards on string which would be worn around the neck. The cards were in three different colors. Red would be allowed in the area for the first hour, green the next hour, and yellow for the last hour. We could at least identify those who were authorized to be in the restricted area and those who were not.

About one hour after sunrise the victims began to pour into the Command Post. They were frustrated and did not want to hear they had to wait until they could be issued entrance passes. Some were beginning to become somewhat violent and had to be removed before the crowd turned into an unruly mob. They all wanted to go inside the area at the same time. We were quickly overwhelmed. I asked for support from the police department and the highway patrol and soon we had more than ample manpower.

We established three lines. Each line was issued one of the three colored entry tags. Of course this meant the other two lines had to wait for the others to clear the area before they were allowed entry so even with a large contingency of law enforcement officers the angry crowd remained aggressive. But after we made a few more arrests the crowd got the message. We did not have any further problems with law and order.

As if the people and rescue workers had not suffered enough it had rained the night before turning the command post area to a sea of mud, making everyone just that more miserable. And to add insult to injury, some of the officers had eaten sandwiches that had been delivered to the Command Post by citizens who wished to help. Unfortunately these sandwiches had been dressed with mayonnaise. The unrefrigerated sandwiches had made them sick. With no restroom facilities available and the pouring rain to contend with I am sure it made for a very long night for some of the sentries.

Photographers and news crews were arriving by the dozens and wanted to shoot footage of the leveled trailer court and the now demolished factory. We told the media we would assign escorts to take small groups into the area, now that it was safe to go in.

Once inside the restricted area many news crews could not believe the raw carnage which lay before them. The mobile homes were so mangled and torn it was impossible to separate one trailer from another. Many of the motor vehicles, which had not been tossed hundreds of yards away, had been totally stripped by the 200 plus mile per hour winds. Many were bare metal where the paint had been beaten away by debris. I took a photograph of one car with a two-by-six inch wooden stud driven in one side and out the other. I still have that photo and I use it when I teach severe weather classes to drive home the point: a car is no place to be in a tornado.

I also took a picture of a large motorcycle which had been tossed more than two blocks. All the spark plug wires were missing as well as many parts from the motor. A Family Bible sat in the middle of an empty field, just north of the mobile home park was not torn or damaged in any way. Clothing, furniture and other furnishings from the mobile home park were scattered as far as the eye could see. One of the more macbre sights was the fiberglass insulation which was everywhere. All the trees which were lucky enough to be left standing appeared to be decorated with the pink insulation, giving the area a strange appearance indeed.

The Kelsey-Hayes Manufacturing Plant looked as if it had been completely gutted by the tornado. A huge gaping hole went completely through the middle of the plant where the monster twister had hit.

The Sedalia Police Department had its firing range just east and north of the Kelsey-Hayes Plant. When we went to the site to assess damages we could not believe our eyes. The back stop some fifty feet long and about ten feet wide which had been constructed with one inch boiler plate was gone. The backstop was so heavy it had to be put in place by a huge crane. We were perplexed. Where had it gone? We walked the once lush field behind the firing range which was now littered with debris looking for the backstop. We found it over a quarter of a mile away. It was twisted so badly it could not be used again. The weight and bulk of this backstop twisted like a piece of spaghetti again reenforced my respect for the fury released by these natural giants. The backstop still sits where the huge tornado had left it seventeen years ago.

To the northeast of our police firing range is another huge factory. It boasted two twin buildings over a quarter of a mile long each. After the 1980 tornado one was completely erased from the face of the earth while the other was left standing unharmed.

Our city received federal assistance from FEMA, the Federal Emergency Management Agency and from SEMA, the State Emergency Management Agency in the form of emergency housing, rebuilding loans and counseling for our residents and emergency responders. Our Sedalia Police Department's Severe Storm Detachment and our local Civil Defense Office learned a great deal following this tornado disaster. Each time emergency response agencies are forced to work together they acquire a collective knowledge of each other's operational capabilities. Disasters are a horrible experience for the victims and for those which must pick up the pieces. If anything good comes from such occurrences it would have to be the experience we gain each time as we work together.

Many people, myself included, take a second look at disasters after the fact to determine what, if anything, could be done the next time to make the overall operation work better. Our Civil Defense Agency coordinated a debriefing after the tornado of May 1980. One of the areas which was not as good as we would wish was communications. This came as no surprise as it always surfaces during mach disaster drill and rehearsals. The problem is communications systems are very expensive and are very easily placed on the back-burner when budgets are prepared. Other than the communications problem the State Emergency Management Agency gave us passing marks or approval.

One thing had puzzled me the day the tornado struck the mobile home park. Officer Rosebrock and I had seen dozens of people running back and forth in the trailer court just minutes before the massive monster leveled sixty mobile homes and pulverized the rest. Very few injuries had been reported from the trailer court and that just did not add up to me.

I learned that over 120 people from the mobile home park had taken shelter in a basement in the home of the trailer court manager, Mr. Heb Harlkess. This explained why we had found no bodies even though the tornado struck the ill–fated mobile home park minutes after we had seen the park residents running around in what looked like a chaotic frenzy. When reporter Phil Goldberg of the Sedalia Democrat asked Harkless what he thought saved the lives of the many people in the trailer court. Harkless said, "I would say it was the coordinated efforts of many people, especially the civil defense, that saved the lives of resident at the trailer park. If it weren't for the hard work of the civil defense, there would have been many deaths."

I would say we owe a great deal to Mr. Harkless. The force of the winds blew one motor vehicle over two blocks from where it was parked and what was left was not worth fixing. When the tornado left he city limits of Sedalia the damage continued. All in all thirty-five farms were heavily damaged and three were totally destroyed. Livestock were killed and injured, most of those which were not killed had broken legs and had to be butchered.

Mrs. Lou Paul, a teacher in Sedalia, recalled her memory of the tornado on May 12, 1980. She recovered from suffered serious injuries and was lucky just to be alive. She told the Sedalia Democrat her story. I found the article which was published on May 15, 1980. It was interesting to me and I thought I would share it with you. The article was entitled *"Sedalia tornadoes 'rain' debris across Missouri* and began, Monday's twisters delivered some Sedalia mail and debris to a farm about 50 miles northeast of here.

"I was standing in bright sunshine-but it was pouring rain-when the stuff started to fall," rural Rocheport, Mo,, farmer Robert Limbach recalled Thursday. "Then it got dead calm, and several sheets of metal roofing, chunks of insulation and pieces of letters and magazines started to fall. We were planting soybeans about 6:16 p.m. and watching for the tornado because we heard the report. It was funny. The roofing was large sheets and it came down like a pinwheel, real slow, graceful as could be."

"About the only identifiable letter was dated February '76. It was a boating safety merit award for Jeff Eugene Loucks," Liimbach said.

Yellow insulation also fell on Columbia's Regional Airport south of the city, a weather expert said Thursday. "It definitely was a by product of Sedalia's tornado," said Grant Darkow, a member of the atmospheric sciences department at the University of Missouri.

Darkow said farmers in the Rocheport area west of Columbia also reported falling debris Monday evening as did people from Clifton City, Pilot Grove and Boonville. All of these cites are miles to the northeast of Sedalia.

On that fateful day of May 12, 1980, Mrs. Paul, educator, wife and mother was in her trailer with her two children preparing dinner. She looked out her window as a sudden wind blew in, and saw a huge tornado near a neighboring farm house about 1/4 mile away. Before she could even walk into the next room to warn her six-year old daughter Julie and her 8 year-old son Rick, the floor in the middle of the trailer raised up and the dwelling snapped in half. The exploding trailer sent the three up in the air depositing them many feet away all in different directions from where the trailer had stood. As the debris fell on them, Mrs. Paul says she was glad to her son call out to her. Then Rick called his sister's name, but she did not answer. Fearing the worst, Rick frantically began to search for his sister. After a horrifying few minutes his sister was located under a pile of debris, shaken, badly injured, but alive.

There are other stories, to numerous to mention, which I keep filed in my desk at home. I make use of these first-hand experiences when I talk with groups concerning tornado safety. To some, tornado safety is a joke, or something not to be concerned about. For these people I make use of my collection of articles and clippings. Not always, but most of the time, these same people suddenly begin to pay attention and even begin to ask questions. In summary, tornados are ruthless killers that unleash their lethality equally and without prejudice. Your best chance to survive one is to understand them and to remain aware of their presence. When warnings are issued, take immediate action. Don't wait until it is to late to take cover.

Chapter Six

Other Thunderstorm Tales

In the previous chapters I have discussed the atrocities and brute strength associated with killer tornados. Although the threat to human life is tremendous another killer lurks among the turmoil in the sky. The National Weather Service says, "At any given time there are roughly 2,000 thunderstorms in progress around the world." Not all of these thunderstorms reach severe limits; however, many do.

Severe thunderstorms present many hazards. High winds can exceed one hundred miles per hour, large damaging hail the size of softballs kill livestock and human beings. Massive amounts of run-off water from high precipitation thunderstorms cause flash flooding and mud slides, all of which kill hundreds of people each year. Micro-bursts, both wet and dry, concentrates all of their power in a downward motion with winds exceeding one hundred miles per hour, flattening anything in their path. Last, but not least, lightning produced from thunderstorms kills over one hundred Americans each year.

The threats associated with severe thunderstorms are many, including the fact that they spawn tornados. The National Weather Service will issue a severe thunderstorm warning should any thunderstorm reach surface wind speeds of 58 miles–per–hour or more, or hail reaching a diameter of 3/4" or larger.

As there are safety tips and guidelines for tornados, there are also tips and guidelines to remember when dealing with severe thunderstorms.

First things first: Be aware of changing weather conditions in your area. An easy way to accomplish this is to monitor your local radio stations. They will be one of the first one to know if severe weather threatens your area. Most likely the Storms Predication Center will issue a severe thunderstorm watch when the conditions are favorable for the development of severe thunderstorms. But remember a thunderstorm can reach severe limits very quickly and there may be no severe thunderstorm watch issued prior to its development.

The watch area is usually issued for a large geographical area, somewhere in the vicinity of 200 miles long and 140 miles wide. As you can see, this area takes in a lot of real estate. The rectangular watch box can be, and often is, reconfigured as the need arises, depending upon the suspected area of developing thunderstorms. Another point to remember: Even if your city or county is outside the watch box area that does not necessarily mean you are safe. The Weather Service includes this fact in its watch text. An excerpt from an actual severe thunderstorm watch states, "Severe thunderstorms, large hail and damaging thunderstorm winds are possible in and close to the watch area." Severe thunderstorm watches will also include specific times when the watch is in effect. The times will vary from watch to watch but as a rule of thumb six to eight hours is not unusual. The severe thunderstorm watch gives you time to make preparations well in advance of an approaching severe thunderstorm.

Severe thunderstorm warnings are issued by local offices of the National Weather Service when the criteria is reached for the thunderstorm to be considered severe. The severe thunderstorm warning means a severe thunderstorm is in your area and you should seek shelter immediately. The severe thunderstorm warning is usually issued for approximately thirty minutes; however, it can be issued for longer periods of time depending upon the thunderstorm threat.

Should a severe thunderstorm warning be issued for your area follow these safety tips.

1. Stay indoors, if possible, and keep informed. Know what the storm is doing. It could produce a tornado. YOUR SHELTERING NEEDS WILL CHANGED DRASTICALLY.

2. Heavy to severe thunderstorms can produce flash flooding. If you live near a creek , river, or small stream, listen for flash flood warnings and be prepared to move out quickly.

3. Lightning is a major threat during severe thunderstorms. Stay away from open doors and windows. Radiators, stoves, and metal pipes and sinks can become conductors for the lightning to enter your shelter. Lightning also targets the tallest features of the landscape, therefore refrain from seeking shelter under trees and tall awnings. Your automobile makes a good shelter from lightning. If you are caught in a thunderstorm inside your car, stay in it but remain aware of the storm. Should a tornado warning be issued or if you see an approaching

tornado, get out immediately and seek shelter in a ditch or ravine.

4. Don't use telephones or electrical equipment during a thunderstorm. The wiring may conduct electricity from a lightning strike. Given the right circumstances severe thunderstorms can cause nearly as much damage as a small tornado. I have reported and experienced hundreds of severe thunderstorms during my time. I know how it feels to be in a van with 95 mile-per-hour winds pushing against the windward side of the vehicle. I have lost many windshields to hail the size of eggs and golf balls. Paint jobs on storm chasing vehicles show the history of the car or truck by the number of dents in the hood and roof from the pelting hail. And I have been struck twice by lightning twice chasing storms across our rolling hills. Each time I had no physical effects from the lightning strikes as I was in my chase vehicle each time, another testimony for the safety of a car in lightning.

Many of the storms had left a lasting impression with my chase partners and me. Some of those memories will stay with me for the rest of my life. They serve to teach us lessons each time they occur. Even the best storm chaser may forget a cardinal rule occasionally. The key is not to forget the right rule at the wrong time. Mother Nature is very unforgiving and some mistakes can cost you your life. One rule you should never forget, do not get too close to a developing or actual tornado. I to have forgotten this rule but by an act of God and a lot of luck I am still here to talk about it.

Some thunderstorms develop so quickly that the National Weather Service Office, and their WSR-88D radars do not have time to issue a warning. By the time the thunderstorm is detected they have grown strong enough to do real damage. Spotters can help in these situations, but even so they must have time to respond. I can remember a particular air-mass thunderstorm which occurred late in the afternoon during the Missouri State Fair. Nineteen fair patrons were injured and dozens of fair employees suffered minor injures due to the storm's wrath. This thunderstorm grew from a small thundershower to severe limits within minutes. It was classified as a high precipitation (HP) single cell thunderstorm. The storm caught the National Weather Service Office and our local Civil Defense Storm Chasers completely by surprise. I will share a story with you.

The Sedalia Police Department decided to enter an exhibit during the 1979 State Fair. The exhibit consisted of a medium sized tent, our Severe Storms Detachment Van, and dozens of other displays inside and around the tent. We manned the exhibit 24 hours a day. One afternoon in the middle of the week, Sergeant Dedrick and I were on duty at the exhibit. That particular day it was a scorching 93 degrees. To add to the misery the humidity was near 50 percent. The only relief was an increasing southernly breeze but the afternoon sun was still very unforgiving.

We noticed clouds starting to gather in the west and we hoped for rain, although Fair Director, Roger Alewele, did not share our hopes. This was understandable. Should heavy thunderstorms assault the fairgrounds the fair would lose many patrons and a considerable amount of income. A sellout crowd would soon be filling the grounds for the evening stage show. No fair director wanted to think about refunding that kind of money.

Still the storm clouds continued to thicken and begin their upward motion high up into the atmosphere. Soon it was apparent we were going to get some relief from the hot sun. I checked with the local Civil Defense Office to see what they were expecting. Normally, I would have been out myself but I could not leave our exhibit at the fair it. Sergeant Dedrick and I could tell the storm was going to grow quickly but we did not know just how severe it would be. However, watching the storm for a few minutes it was very clear to us it would track in our direction. During the Missouri State Fair the National Weather Service Office in Columbia, Missouri kept extra watch over our skies since it was not uncommon for 30,000 people to be on the grounds during the day. The Missouri State Fair has always been agriculturally based for the most part so most of the exhibits, displays, and events were outside, leaving most of the fair vulnerable to the elements and the weather. This storm took the National Weather Service Office totally by surprise.

It began as a small thundershower in the southwestern portion of Pettis County, only ten miles away from the fair grounds. By the time the radar operator located the small cell it had grown into a full fledged thunderstorm in a matter of minutes.

Whiteman Air Force Base, just fifteen miles to our west, is much closer than Columbia, Missouri which is eighty miles to our east. The radar operator at Whiteman Air Force Base was contacted by one of their security patrols which were out checking on the missile silos about five miles southwest of the fair grounds. They gave the radar operator their radio report concerning the deteriorating weather conditions.

Rene and I began to take as many of our exhibits inside the tent as possible. It was clear we would be under the gun in about ten minutes. We prepared for the worst. The thunder was getting much louder now and the lightning strikes were increasing by the minute. We could feel the cooler air arriving from the rain shaft which lay only a few miles to our west. I have to admit, it was a welcomed relief from the searing sun; however, at the same time I had a very bad feeling over what was yet to come.

I estimated there were around 25,000 people on the grounds that afternoon. I also knew there was no way we shelter that many people.

I remember the outdoor public address system announcer advising the fair patrons of the approaching potentially dangerous storm. He did not tell them to leave the grounds but he did say high winds heavy rain and frequent lightning strikes were associated with the storm. The announcement was enhanced by the thunder and lightning in the background. I believe most of the people visiting the fair took this warning very seriously.

Rene and I finished driving the tent stakes into the ground as far as we could. We unplugged all the electrical wires and broke out our first aid kits, should we need them after the storm. There was not much else we could actually do but wait it out. The wait was not a long one. The storm was now just entering the western end of the fair, where the mile–long midway attractions were located. We could see a wall of water sweeping in from the west across the midway. There were dozens of lightning ground strikes per minute, some of them striking within a few feet of our tent.

The last few minutes before the storm arrived were nerve racking. This storm meant business.

In a flash the rain began a downpour which left us huddling against the walls of the tent. The rain swept in a near horizontal plane swept in by the winds of the severe thunderstorm. The parched ground instantly turned into thick mud. The winds increased by the second until they reached 75 to 80 miles per hour. The few people who were still outside were actually being pushed to the ground by the ferocious wind. Two children suddenly bolted into our tent. Rene and I put them behind a large display board to shield them from the driving rain. They could not be more than nine or ten and were scared half out of their wits. The winds were so strong, the tent poles on the inside of the tent were being lifted from the ground. Rene and I each grabbed onto one pole in an attempt to keep the tent from blowing away. But The power of this storm was so tremendous, Rene and I were lifted off the ground as we desperately clung to the poles.

Then as if the winds, rain, and lightning were not enough it began to hail, Small hail at first then golf ball size. We immediately lay the children down and put the wooden exhibit board over them to keep them from injury. It hailed for about two minutes. As the hail and rain subsided Rene and I were getting really worried. We feared there was a funnel cloud or tornado at our doorstep. A tornado at that time of day on the Missouri State Fair Grounds would be catastrophic. We quickly checked on the children then went outside the tent to look for signs of a funnel cloud or tornado as the rain free base was now right over head. We did not see anything which resembled a funnel cloud or tornado. That was a relief. But what we did see was bad enough.

The high winds had caught the Double Farris Wheel ride operator by surprise. He did not have enough time to get everyone off of the carnival ride before the storm had hit. Two people were stuck over 90 feet in the air. The ride operator could not get them down due to an electrical outage. They had actually ridden out the storm in a tiny swinging seat of the Double Farris Wheel.

Nineteen people were injured from the effects of the thunderstorm that afternoon. Some were bruised and cut from the large hail. Many received lacerations from flying debris. Only a handful of the injured persons required medical treatment at Bothwell Regional Health Center, but, even those few were too many as far as we were concerned.

The Missouri State Highway Patrol and the State Fair Security Force began to implement their emergency plan. One of the main hazards following a storm of this magnitude is exposed electrical lines. Scores of them problems were everywhere. Standing water and exposed electrical wires is not a good combination. It took hours to restore the power and during this time it took hundreds of state fair employees to secure them until it was safe.

The top of the Show-Me Arena was completely destroyed. Not a single tent or awning in the midway was left standing. Tons of small debris were piled against the grandstand entrance, everything from small stuffed animals to boxes of merchandise from the venders across the street. I do remember seeing a base drum and a snare drum piled against the fencing near the main ticket office. I learned later the instruments had rolled over two blocks from where they were originally located. Two of the fair's larger tents went down causing a considerable amount of damage to the contents inside. Overall, the emergency response agencies on the grounds did an excellent job. Prior planning made the difference. Fair Director Roger Alewele and rest of the staff were very thankful the severe thunderstorm did not produce a tornado as had the thunderstorm during the fair of 1952.

Occasionally a tornado chaser is totally amazed by the sheer magnitude and raw power of nature. My chase partners and I were absolutely awestruck by a phenomenon which very few of our peers are lucky enough to witness. I remember such a chase which proved to be the most unique tornado experience I have had to this day.

One muggy spring evening in 1982, Jess Masscarenaz, at that time our Deputy Civil Defense Director for Pettis County, called me about a potential severe weather situation intensifying near by. He said he was going to activate our Civil Defense Storm Chasers around 6:00 p.m. Jess had received information a strong thunderstorm system was moving our way from eastern Kansas. I called Sergeant Rene Dedrick and asked him if he were going out with me to spot this system. Rene said he would meet me at police headquarters.

When we arrived wo made sure the radio operator knew we were going to deploy and advised the on-duty shift commander of the situation. The shift commander was already on top of the situation. He had overheard radio traffic in Johnson County, Missouri indicating the thunderstorm was now at severe limits just west of them. No tornados had been reported at that time by the Johnson County Sheriff's Department or the Missouri State Highway Patrol.

Rene and I jumped into our van and headed west. We stationed ourselves just south of the west city limits hoping we could see the back of the approaching thunderstorms. Jess came up on the civil defense channel and told us he had received information that the thunderstorm tops were already nearing fifty-five thousand feet. This told us the thunderstorms were most likely going to pack large hail and high winds. Although the National Weather Service had not yet issued any kind of severe watch we knew what lay ahead.

The police radio operator called and told Rene and me that the National Weather Service Office in Columbia, Missouri had issued a severe thunderstorm warning for Johnson County, Missouri. We could tell the storm was going to be a good one as we watched a dazzling light show just west of us in Johnson County. After twenty minutes or so the storm entered the westernmost portion of Pettis County. We could hear the faint rolling of thunder in the distance. It was not long before the thunder was crashing much closer. On occasion, you could hear the sizzling sound of a stray ground strike hitting close to us followed and then a jolting clap of thunder.

The storm was now edging its way towards our city. The Sedalia Police Department Radio Operator called us. She said the National Weather Service had issued a severe thunderstorm warning for Sedalia and Pettis County. We quickly relayed this information to Jess and the Emergency Operations Center downtown, on the Civil Defense radio channel.

Jess moved some of the other spotters farther to the south and west to get a better view of the thunderstorm's back side. They were moving from west-southwest to east-northeast at 35 miles per hour. Rene and I moved back toward town to a hill top in the northwestern part of town where there were not many lights.

Civil defense spotters just five miles west of our location were reporting surface winds near 70 miles-per-hour, and hail the size of golf balls. Extremely heavy rain was coming down in pelting sheets. After listening to the radio traffic on the civil defense radio, Rene and I decided to head our van into the wind. Our van was very top heavy and we were afraid the winds would increase in velocity and strike us broadside, not a good thing for the folks inside. Also I was sure the chief would not be thrilled with a repair bill of that size.

We turned the van head-on into where we thought the wind would be coming from and we waited for the severe thunderstorm to unleash it's power on the city. As the storm approached our area we were hit by a gust front wind which shook the van and made it veer from side to side violently. Apparently the winds had increased as we had suspicioned. After the initial gust front, and without haste, the rain began to buffet our van with a terrible fury. The rain drops were some of the largest I had ever seen and the estimated 85 mile-per-hour wind made it impossible to see anything at all. We knew our position was not a good one. Should a tornado or funnel cloud be associated with this storm, it would most likely immediately follow the heavy rain and hail. But, like I said before, sometimes things don't happen the way you plan. The hail that began to crash into our van was marble sized and growing. Before it disappeared it had grown to the size of golf balls. All along the roadside were thick white deposits of hail, some of them six inches deep.

When the hail and wind subsided we quickly put our van into motion. We overheard Jess break the silence on the Civil Defense radio. We could not copy his transmission completely, because the lightning was causing an extreme amount of static but I thought I heard him report a tornado on the ground. Rene and I turned up the volume on the CD radio and told him to repeat his traffic. I was right. Jess told us a tornado was on the ground approximately three miles west of our location. He said it was a big one. Jess believed it was moving northeast but he could not tell how fast it was moving. We told Jess we would wait for him at our location then assist him in chasing the tornado for plotting purposes.

A few minutes after Jess reported the tornado the National Weather Service Office contacted the police radio operator over the NAWAS line. They confirmed what our storm chasers were reporting and issued a tornado warning for the northern half of Pettis County. The outdoor warning sirens were activated and emergency operations plans put into effect. As the sirens blasted away we impatiently waited for Jess. We also kept looking out the window up and over our van every now and then. It would not be the first time a funnel cloud developed over one of our spotters.

Soon the storm was nearly away from the city and there we were smack dab in the middle of the rain free base. In the absence of the rain and hail it was now possible to see what was behind the potent thunderstorm. The wind suddenly died down. We knew the tornado was very, very close. Jess arrived and told us we should be able to see the tornado by now. We exited our vehicles to get a better look. The lightning was tremendous which almost made us thank twice about getting out of the van, but we had to get out of the vehicle to get a better look. The tornado was there, we just did not know exactly where. Jess, Rene, and I all instinctively looked in the same direction, waiting for a lightning flash to illuminate the cloud formations. It did not take long. When the lightning did flash in the right spot we got the shock and view a storm chaser would kill for. Not only was there a huge tornado on the ground, there were three other smaller tornados on the ground following the parent tornado. The entire string of tornados was about two miles long and moving east-northeast.

We immediately relayed this information to the cities in our northern and eastern county. Hughesville, Houstonia, and Long Wood were all in danger. Our adjoining counties to the north and east were also contacted by our emergency operations center. We did not know how long the tornados were going to stay on the ground, but it was no time to take chances.

We decided to follow the tornados until they left our jurisdiction. We were hoping the four tornados would miss our smaller cities to the north and east. We must have been living right! The tornados did miss the three towns which were in harms way, although a few farm homes and out buildings did experience some damage. No injuries, just damage. And, don't forget. Four tornados were on the ground! I got the feeling the Saline and Boone

County storm chasers did not believe our report of the quad-tornados. We followed the quad-tornados for 18 miles until they reached Interstate I-70. Then Saline County Civil Defense spotters took over and we returned to Sedalia. Their radio channels really started to pop when they saw the four tornados we had reported. We could only chuckle.

Once in town we could not resist the temptation to tell the rest of the other spotters what we had seen. I have seen multi-vortexes before, but, never have I seen four separate tornados on the ground at one time, in a series. I feel fortunate to have had the opportunity to observe such a phenomenon. It was an event none of us would never forget the rest of our lives.

Late spring and summer of 1980 was an active year for severe storms in and around the west central Missouri area. We had survived many severe thunderstorm and tornado watches, some of which included near misses from visiting funnel clouds and/or tornados. We were still in the recovery stage from the May 1980 tornado which took out our northwest corner of town. Our spotters had earned a healthy respect from other regional spotter groups and Weather Service officials.

The Pettis County Civil Defense Agency went through some changes in the early 80's. The city of Sedalia and the county of Pettis decided it would be best if the agency were jointly funded to enhance their effectiveness. The new name was the Sedalia-Pettis County Emergency Management Agency (EMA). The name change was necessary for many reasons. The old name of Civil Defense really originated from the war days and the cold war with the Soviet Union. Its main function was to provide support to the population should a thermonuclear war between the two super powers become a reality. Today EMA is run by Director, Bill Michael. We will always support our volunteer storm chasers and they remain ready to perform their duty well into the new millennium. Our EMA also is responsible for enhanced 911 (E-911) mapping and addressing for our county which is a full time job in itself. Also we maintain all the records for federal and state programs which pertain to hazardous chemicals stored and used by local industries. Last, but not least, we are charged with emergency warning and the coordination of all city-county emergency response agencies and the mach disaster rehearsals we conduct each year. The agency has changed roles over the years but its foundation remains the same: its corps of volunteers.

Bibliography

Abernethy, James "Tornado Protection-selecting and designing safe areas in buildings" *FEMA* OCT 1982

Braden, Don "Twister" *Sedalia Democrat* 4 May 1997 P. 5A

Cowan, Ronald "Editor's Mail-More tales of twister" *Sedalia Democrat* 18 May 1977

Daniels, Pete "Friday's severe weather leaves wide destruction"*Sedalia Democrat* 22 Apr. 1973 P.1

Goldberg, Phil "No deaths called "miracle" by some *Sedalia Democrat* 15 May 1980

Jennings, Ron "Remembering the Rebuilding" *Sedalia Democrat* 4 MAY 1997 P.1

Marsh, Vicki "Forty Injured in Storm; None Serious" *Sedalia Democrat* 6 May 1977 P. 1

Mosier,Tim Anonymous Interview 8 Aug 1996

National Weather Association "Glossary of Weather Terms," Washington D.C. 1993

National Weather Service "Advanced Spotters Guide" NOAA PA 92055 P 5

National Weather Service "Advanced Spotters Guide" NOAA PA 92055 P16

Sedalia Democrat "Through the storm count your blessings" 6 May 1997

Sedalia Democrat "Computer card here found in Moberly" 5 Sep. 1977

Sedalia Democrat "Title Unknown" 3 June 1977

Stacy, Harriet "Lou Paul Recalls May 12, 1980" *Sedalia Democrat* Date unknown

Vaughan, Ed "Early warning given credit" *Sedalia Democrat* 5 May 1977

Glossary of Terms

A

AC Convective outlook issued by the Storms Prediction Center. Abbreviation for Anticipated Convections.

AltoCumulus CAStellanus ACCAS mid-level clouds, generally 8 to 15 thousand feet, of which at least a fraction of their upper parts show development. These clouds often are taller than they are wide, giving them a turret-shaped appearance.

Accessory Cloud A cloud which is dependent on a larger cloud system for development and continuance. Roll clouds and wall clouds are examples of accessory clouds.

Advection Transport of an atmospheric property by the wind

161

Air-Mass Thunderstorm Generally, a thunderstorm not associated with a front or other type of synoptic-scale forcing mechanism. Air-Mass thunderstorms typically are associated with warm, humid air in the summer months; they develop during the afternoon in response to insolation, and dissipate rather quickly after sunset. Generally they are less severe than other types of thunderstorms, but they still are capable of producing downbursts, brief heavy rain, and (in extreme cases) hail over 3/4 inch in diameter. Since all thunderstorms are associated with some type of forcing mechanism, a synoptic-scale or otherwise, the existence of true air-mass thunderstorms is debatable. Therefore, the term is somewhat controversial and should be used with discretion.

Algorithm A computer program, or set of programs, which is designed to systematically solve a certain kind of problem. WSR-88D radars (NEXRAD) employ algorithms to analyze radar data and automatically determine storm motion, probability of hail, VIL, accumulated rainfall, and several other parameters.

Anticyclonic Rotation Rotation in the opposite sense as the earth's rotation, i.e., clockwise in the northern hemisphere as would be seen from above. The opposite of cyclonic rotation.

Anvil The flat, spreading top of a CB (cumulonimbus), often shaped like an anvil. Thunderstorm anvils may spread hundreds of miles downwind from the thunderstorm itself, and sometimes may spread upwind(see back-sheared anvil).

Anvil Crawler [slang] A lightning discharge occurring within the anvil of a thunderstorm, characterized by one or more channels that appear to crawl along the underside of the anvil. They typically appear during the weakening or dissipating stage of the parent thunderstorm, or an active MCS.

Anvil Dome A large overshooting top or penetrating tip.

Anvil Rollover [slang] A circular or semicircular lip of clouds along the underside of the upwind part of a back-sheared anvil, indicating rapid expansion of the anvil. (See *cumuliform anvil, knuckles, mushroom*).

Anvil Zits [slang] Frequent, often continuous or nearly continuous, localized lightning discharges occurring within a thunderstorm anvil.

Anomalous Propagation (AP) Radar term for false (non-precipitation) echoes resulting from nonstandard propagation of the radar beam under certain atmospheric conditions.

Approaching (severe levels) A thunderstorm which contains winds of 35 to 49 knots (40-57 mph), or hail at least one inch but less than 3/4 in diameter. (See *severe thunderstorm*).

Arcus A low, horizontal cloud formation associated with the leading edge of thunderstorm outflow i.e., the gust front. Roll clouds and shelf clouds both are types of arcus clouds.

AViatioN model AVN one of the operational forecast models that run a NCEP. The AVN is run four times daily, at 0000, 0600,1200, and 1800 GMT. As of fall 1996, forecast output was available operationally out to 72 hours only from the 0000 and 1200 runs. At 0600 and 1800, the model is run only out to 54 hours.

B

Back-Building Thunderstorm A thunderstorm in which new development takes place on the upwind side (usually the west or southwest side), giving the impression that the storm is remaining stationary or propagating in a backward direction.

Backing Winds Winds which shift in a counterclockwise direction with time at a given location (e.g. from southerly to southeasterly), or that change direction in a counterclockwise sense with height (e.g., westerly at the surface but becoming more southerly aloft); the opposite of veering winds.

In storm spotting, a backing wind usually refers to the turning of a south or southwest surface wind to a more east or southeasterly direction. Backing of the surface wind can increase the potential for tornado development by increasing the direction shear at low levels.

Back-Sheared Anvil [slang] A thunderstorm anvil which spreads upwind, against the flow aloft. A back-sheared anvil often implies a very strong updraft and a high severe weather potential.

Barber Pole [slang] A thunderstorm updraft with a visual appearance that includes cloud striations curved like the stripes of a barber pole. The structure typically is most pronounced on the leading edge of the updraft, while drier air from the rear flank down draft often erodes the clouds on the trailing side of the updraft.

Baroclinic Zone A region in which a temperature gradient exists on a constant pressure surface. Barocliinic zones are favored areas for strengthening and weakening systems; barotropic systems, on the other hand, do not exhibit significant changes in intensity. Also, wind shear is characteristic of a baroclinic zone.

Barotropic System A weather system in which temperature and pressure surfaces are coincident, i.e., temperature is uniform (no temperature gradient) on a constant pressure surface. Barotropic systems are characterized by a lack of wind shear, and thus are generally unfavorable areas for severe thunderstorm development. See baroclinic zone.

Usually, in operational meteorology, references to barotropic systems refer to equivalent barotropic systems, systems in which temperature gradients exist, but are parallel to height gradients on a constant pressure surface. In such systems, height contours and isotherms are parallel everywhere, and winds do not change direction with height.

As a rule, a true equivalent barotropic system can never be achieved in the real atmosphere. While some systems (such as closed lows or cutoff lows) may reach a state that is close to equivalent barotropic, the term barotropic system usually is used in a relative sense to describe systems that are really only close to being equivalent barotropic, i.e., isotherms and height contours are nearly parallel everywhere and directional wind shear is weak.

Bear's Cage [slang] A region of storm-scale rotation, in a thunderstorm, which is wrapped in heavy precipitation. This area often coincides with a radar hook echo and/or mesocyclone, especially one associated with an HP storm.

Beaver's Tail [slang] A particular tupe of inflow band with a relatively broad, flat appearance sugestive of a beaver's tail. It is attached to a supercell's general updraft and is oriented roughly parallel to the pseudo-warm front, i.e., usually east to west or southeast to northwest. As with any inflow band, the strength of the inflow changes, See also inflow-stinger.

Spotters should note the distinction between a beaver tail and a tail cloud. A tail cloud typically is attached to the wall cloud and has a cloud base at about the same level as the wall cloud itself. A beaver tail, on the other hand, is not attached to the wall cloud and has a cloud base at about the same height as the updraft-base (which by definition is higher than the wall cloud). Unlike the beaver tail, the tail cloud forms from air that is flowing from the storm's main precipitation cascade region (or outflow region). Thus, it can be oriented at a large angle to the pseudo-warm front.

Blue Watch or Blue Box [slang] A severe thunderstorm watch.

Boundary Layer In general, a layer of air adjacent to a bounding surface. Specifically, the term most often refers to the *planetary boundary layer*, which is the layer within which the effects of friction are significant. For the earth, this layer is considered to be roughly the lowest one or two kilometers of the atmosphere. It is within this layer that temperatures are most strongly affected by daytime insolation and nightime radiational cooling, and winds are affected by friction with the earth's surface. The effects of friction die out gradually with height, so the "top" of this layer can not be defined exactly.

There is a thin layer immediately above the earth's surface known as the *surface boundary layer,* or simply the surface layer. This layer is only a part of the planetary boundary layer, and represents the layer within which friction effects are more or less constant throughout (as opposed to decreasing with height, as they do above it). The surface boundary layer is roughly ten meters thick, but again the exact depth is indeterminate. Like friction , the effects of insolation and radiational cooling are strongest within this layer.

Bow Echo A radar echo which is linear but bent outward in a bow shape. Damaging straight-line winds often occur near the "crest" or center of a bow echo. Areas of circulation can also develop at either end of a bow echo, which sometimes can lead to tornado formation-especially in the left (usually northern) end, where the circulation exhibits cyclonic rotation.

Box (or Watch Box) [slang] A severe thunderstorm or tornado watch BRN see Bulk Richardson Number

Bubble High A mesoscale area of high pressure, typically associated with cooler air from the rainy downdraft area of a thunderstorm or a complex of thunderstorms. A gust front or outflow boundary separates a bubble high from the surrounding air.

Bulk Richardson Number (BRN) A non-dimensional number relating to vertical stability and vertical shear, generally, stability divided by shear. High values indicate unstable and/or weakly-sheared environments; low values indicate weak instability and/or strong vertical shear. Generally, values in the range of around 50 to 100 suggest environmental conditions favorable for supercell development.

Bust [slang] An inaccurate forecast or an unsuccessful storm chase, usually a situation in which thunderstorms or severe weather are expected, but do not occur.

Bounded Weak Echo Region BWER also known as a vault Radar signature within a thunderstorm characterized by a local minimum in radar reflectivity at low levels which extend upward into, and is surrounded by, higher reflectivities aloft. This feature is associated with a strong updraft and is almost always found in the inflow region of a thunderstorm. It cannot be seen visually.

C
Cloud-to-Air CA lightning

Cap (or Capping Inversion) A layer of relatively warm air aloft (usually several thousand feet above the ground) which suppresses or delays the development of thunderstorms. Air parcels rising into this layer become cooler than the surrounding air, which inhibits their ability to rise further. As such, the cap often prevents or delays thunderstorm development even in the presence of extreme instability. However if the cap is removed or weakened, then explosive thunderstorm development can occur.

The cap is an important ingredient in most severe thunderstorm episodes, as it serves to separate warm moist air below and cooler, drier air above. With the cap in place, air can continue to warm and/or moisten, thus increasing the amount of potential instability. Or, air above it can cool, which also increase potential instability. But without a cap, either process (warming/moistening at low levels or cooling aloft) results in a faster release of available instablility-often before instability levels become large enough to support severe weather development.

Convective Available Potential Energy CAPE A measure of the amount of energy available for convection. CAPE is directly related to the maximum potential vertical speed within an updraft, thus, higher values indicate greater potential for severe weather. Observed values in thunderstorm environments often may exceed 1,000 joules per kilogram (j/kg) and in extreme cases may exceed 5,000 j/kg. However, as with other indices or indicators, there are no threshold values above which severe weather becomes imminent. CAPE is represented on a sounding by the area enclosed between the environmental temperature profile and the path of a rising air parcel, over the layer within which the later is warmer than the former. This area often is called positive area.

Cb-Cumulonimbus Cloud Characterized by the strong vertical development in the form of mountains or huge towers topped at least partially by a smooth, flat, often fibrous anvil. Also known colloquially as a *thunderhead.*

CC-Cloud-to-Cloud lightning Cell-Convection in the form of single updraft, down draft, or updraft/down draft couplet, typically seen as a vertical come or tower as in a cumulus or towering cumulus cloud. A typical thunderstorm consists of several cells.

The term "cell" also is used to describe the radar echo returned by an individual shower or thunderstorm. Such usage, although common, is technically incorrect.

CG-Cloud-to-Ground lightning flash.

Chaff Small strips of metal foil, usually dropped in large quantities from aircraft or balloons. Chaff typically produces a radar echo which closely resembles precipitation. Chaff drops once were conducted by the military in order to confuse enemy radar, but now are conducted mainly for radar testing and calibration purposes.

Convective INhibition CIN A measure of the amount of energy needed in order to initiate convection.

Values of CIN typically reflect the strength of the cap. They are obtained on a sounding by computing the area enclosed between the environmental temperature profile and the path of a rising air parcel, over the layer within which the latter is cooler than the former. (This area sometimes is called negative area.)

Cirrus-High-Level Clouds, 16,000 feet or more, Composed of ice crystals and appearing in the form of white, delicate filaments or white or mostly white patches or narrow bands. Cirrus clouds typically have a fibrous, or hairlike, appearance, and often are semi-transparent. Thunderstorm anvils are a form of cirrus cloud, but most cirrus clouds are not associated with thunderstorms

Classic Supercell See *supercell.*

Clear Slot A local region of clearing skies or reduced cloud cover, indicating an intrusion of drier air; often seen as a bright area with higher cloud bases on the west or southwest side of a wall cloud. A clear lot is believed to be a visual indication of a rear flank down draft.

Closed Low A low pressure area with a distinct center of cyclonic rotation which can be completely encircled by one or more isobars or height contour lines. The term is usually used to distinguish a low pressure area aloft from a low-pressure trough. Closed Lows aloft typically are partially or completely detached from the main westerly current, and thus move relatively slowly.

Cloud Streets Rows of cumulus or cumulus-type clouds aligned parallel to the low-level flow. Cloud streets sometimes can be seen from the ground, but are seen best on satellite photographs.

Cloud Tags Ragged, detached cloud fragments; fractus or scud.

Cold Advection Transport of cold air into a region by horizontal winds.

Cold Pool A region of relatively cold air, represented on a weather map analysis as a relative minimum in temperature surrounded by closed isotherms. Cold Pools aloft represent regions of relatively low stability, while surface-based Cold Pools are regions of relatively stable air.

Collar Cloud A generally circular ring of cloud that may be observed on rare occasions surrounding the upper part of a wall cloud. This term sometimes is used incorrectly as a synonym for wall cloud.

Comma Cloud A synoptic scale cloud pattern with a characteristic comma- like shape, often seen on satellite photographs associated with large and intense low-pressure systems.

Condensation Funnel A funnel-shaped cloud associated with rotation and consisting of condensed water droplets (as opposed to smoke, dust, debris, etc). Compare with debris cloud.

Confluence A pattern of wind flow in which air flows inward toward an axis oriented parallel to the general direction of flow. It is the opposite of difluence. Confluence is not the same as convergence. Winds often accelerate as they enter a confluent zone, resulting in speed divergence which offsets the (apparent) converging effect of the confluent flow.

Congestus or Cumulus Congestus Same as towering cumulus.

Convection Generally, transport of heat and moisture by the movement of a fluid. In meteorology, the term specifically describes vertical transport of heat and moisture, especially by updrafts and down drafts in an unstable atmosphere. The terms *convection* and *thunderstorms* often are used interchangeably, although thunderstorms are only one form of convection. Cbs, towering cumulus clouds, and ACCAS clouds all are visible forms of convection; however, convection is not always made visible by clouds. Convection which occurs without cloud formation is called dry convection, while the visible convection processes referred to above are forms of moist convection.

Convective Outlook, sometimes called AC A forecast containing the area(s) of expected thunderstorm occurrence and expected severity over the contiguous United States, issued several times daily by the SPC. The terms *approaching, slight risk, moderate risk* and *high risk* are used to describe severe thunderstorm potential. Local versions sometimes are prepared by local NWS offices.

Convective Temperature The approximate temperature that the air near the ground must warm to for surface-based convection to develop, based on analysis of a sounding.

Calculation of the convective temperature involves many assumptions, such as, thunderstorms sometimes develop well before or well after the convective temperature is reached (or may not develop at all). However, in some cases the convective temperature is a useful parameter for forecasting the onset of convection.

Convergence A contraction of a vector field; the opposite of divergence. Convergence in a horizontal wind field indicates that more air is entering a given area than is leaving. To compensate for the resulting "excess," vertical motion may result: upward forcing if convergence is at low levels, or downward forcing (subsidence) if convergence is at high levels. Upward forcing from low-level convergence increases the potential for thunderstorm development (when other factors, such as instability, are favorable). Compare with confluence.

Core Punch [slang] Penetration of a vehicle into the heavy precipitation core of a thunderstorm. Core punching is not a recommended procedure for storm spotting.

Cumuliform Anvil A thunderstorm anvil with visual characteristics   resembling   cumulus-type clouds(rather than the more typical fibrous appearance associated with cirrus). A cumuliform anvil arises from rapid spreading of a thunderstorm updraft, and thus implies a very strong updraft. See *Anvil Rollover.*

Cumulus Detached clouds, generally dense and with sharp outlines showing vertical development in the form of domes, mounds, or towers. Tops normally are rounded, while bases are more horizontal. See *Cb, towering cumulus.*

Cumulus Congestus or Congestus Same as towering cumulus.

Cutoff low A closed low which has become completely displaced (cut off) from basic westerly current, and moves independently of that current. Cutoff lows may remain nearly stationary for days, or on occasion may move westward opposite to the prevailing flow aloft, i.e., retrogression.

Cutoff low and *closed low* often are used interchangeably to describe low pressure centers aloft. However, not all closed lows are completely removed from the influence of the basic westerlies. Therefore, the recommended usage of the terms is to reserve the use of *cutoff low* to those closed lows which clearly are detached completely from the westerlies.

Cyclic Storm A thunderstorm that undergoes cycles of intensification and weakening (pulses) while maintaining its individuality. Cyclic supercells are capable of producing multiple tornadoes (i.e., tornado family) and/or several bursts of severe weather. A storm which undergoes only one cycle (pulse), and then dissipates, is known a pulse storm.

Cyclogenesis Development or intensification of a low-pressure center (cyclone).

Cyclonic Circulation or Cyclonic Rotation Circulation (or rotation) which is in the same sense as the earth's rotation, i.e., counter clockwise (in the Northern Hemisphere) as would be seen from above. Nearly all meso cyclones and strong or violent tornadoes exhibit cyclonic rotation, but some smaller vortices, such as gustnadoes, occasionally rotate anticyclonically (clockwise). Compare with anticyclonic rotation.

D

dBZ-Nondimensional "unit" of radar reflectivity which represents a logarithmic power ration (in decibels or dB) with respect to radar reflectivity factor, Z.

The value of Z is a function of the amount of radar beam energy that is back scattered by a target and detected as a signal (or echo). Higher values of Z (and dBZ) thus indicate more energy being back scattered by a target. The amount of back scattered energy generally is related to precipitation intensity, such that higher values of dBZ that are detected from precipitation areas generally indicates higher precipitation rates. However, other factors can affect reflectivity, such as width of the radar beam, precipitation type, drop size, or the presence of ground clutter of AP WSR-88D radars can detect reflectivities as low as -32 dBZ near the radar site, but significant (measurable) precipitation generally is indicated by reflectivities of around 15 dBZ or more. Values of 50 dBZ or more, normally are associated with heavy thunderstorms, perhaps with hail, but as with most other quantities, there are no reliable threshold values associated with each VIP level.

Debris Cloud A rotating "cloud" of dust or debris, near or on the ground, often appearing beneath a condensation funnel and surrounding the base of a tornado.

This term is similar to dust whirl, although the latter typically refers to a circulation which contains dust but not necessarily any debris. A dust plume, on the other hand, does not rotate. Note that a debris cloud appearing beneath a thunderstorm will confirm the presence of a tornado, even in the absence of a condensation funnel.

Delta T A simple representation of the mean lapse rate within a layer of the atmosphere, obtained by calculating the difference between observed temperatures at the bottom and top of the layer. Delta Ts often are computed operationally over the layer between pressure levels of 700 mb and 500 mb, in order to evaluate the amount of instability in mid-levels of the atmosphere. Generally, values greater than about 18 indicate sufficient instability for severe thunderstorm development.

Derecho (day-RAY-cho) A widespread and usually fast-moving windstorm associated with convection. Derechos include any family of down burst clusters produced by an extra tropical MCS and can produce damaging straight-line winds over hundreds of miles long and more than 100 miles across.

Dew Point or Dew-point Temperature A measure of atmospheric moisture. It is the temperature to which air must be cooled in order to reach saturation, assuming air pressure and moisture content are constant.

Differential Motion Cloud motion that appears to differ relative to other nearby cloud elements, e.g., clouds moving from left to right relative to other clouds in the foreground or background. Cloud rotation is one example of differential motion, but not all differential motion indicates rotation. For example, horizontal wind shear along a gust front may result in differential cloud motion without the presence of rotation.

Difluence or Diffluence A pattern of wind flow in which air moves outward in a "fan-out" pattern away from a central axis that is oriented parallel to the general direction of the flow. It is the opposite of confluence.

Difluence in an upper level wind field is considered a favorable condition for severe thunderstorm development, if other parameters are also favorable. But difluence is not the same as divergence. In a diffluent flow, winds normally decelerate as they move through the region of difluence, resulting in speed convergence which offsets the apparent diverging effect of the diffluent flow.

Directional Shear The component of wind shear which is due to a change in wind direction with height, e.g., southeasterly winds at the surface and southwesterly winds aloft. A veering with height in the lower part of the atmosphere is a type of directional shear often considered important for tornado development.

Diurnal Daily Related to actions which are completed in the course of a calendar day, and which typically recur every calendar day, e.g., *diurnal* temperature rises during the day, and falls at night.

Divergence The expansion or spreading out of a vector field; usually said of horizontal winds. It is the opposite of convergence. Divergence at the upper levels of the atmosphere enhances upward motion, and hence the potential for thunderstorm development, if other factors are favorable.

Dopplar Radar Radar that can measure radial velocity, the instantaneous component of motion parallel to the radar beam i.e., toward or away from the radar antenna.

Downburst A strong downdraft resulting in an outward burst of damaging winds on or near the ground. Downburst's winds can produce damage similar to a strong tornado. Although usually associated with thunderstorms, downbursts can occur with showers too weak to produce thunder. See *dry* and *wet microburst.*

Downdraft A small-scale column of air that rapidly sinks toward the ground, usually accompanied by precipitation as in a shower or thunderstorm. A downburst is the result of a strong downdraft.

Downstream In the same direction as a stream or other flow, or toward the direction in which the flow is moving.

Dry Adiabat A line of constant potential temperature on a thermodynamic chart.

Dry Line A boundary separating moist and dry air masses, and an important factor in severe weather frequency in the Great Plains. It typically lies north-south across the central and southern high plains states during the spring and early summer, where it separates moist air from the Gulf of Mexico to the east, and dry desert air from the southwestern states to the west. The dry line typically advances eastward during the afternoon and retreats westward at night. However, a strong storm system can sweep the dry line eastward into the Mississippi Valley, or even further east, regardless of the time of day. A typical dry line passage results in a sharp drop in humidity, hence the name, clearing skies, and a wind shift from south or southeasterly to west or southwesterly. Blowing dust and rising temperatures also may follow, especially if the dry line passes during the daytime; see *dry punch*).

These changes occur in reverse order when the

dry line retreats westward. Severe and sometimes tornadic thunderstorms often develop along a dry line or in the moist air just to the east of it, especially when it begins moving eastward. See *LP storm.*

Dry-line Bulge A bulge in the dry line, representing the area where dry air is advancing most strongly at lower levels i.e., a surface dry punch. Severe weather potential is increased near and ahead of a dry-line bulge.

Dry-line Storm Generally, any thunderstorm that develops on or near a dry- line. The term often is used synonymously with LP storm, since the latter almost always occurs near the dry line.

Dry Microburst A microburst with little or no precipitation reaching the ground; most common in semi-arid regions. It may or may not produce lightning. Dry microbursts may develop in an otherwise fair-weather pattern; visible signs may include a cumulus cloud or small Cb with a high base and high-level virga., or perhaps only an orphan anvil from a dying rain shower. At the ground, the only visible sign might be a dust plume or a ring of blowing dust beneath a local area of virga. Compare with *wet microburst.*

Dry Punch [slang] A surge of drier air; normally a synoptic-scale or mesoscale process. A dry punch at the surface results in a dry line bulge. A dry punch aloft above an area of moist air at the low levels often increases the potential for severe weather.

Dry Slot A zone of dry and relatively cloud-free air which wraps east-or northeastward into the southern and eastern parts of a synoptic scale or mesoscale low pressure system. A dry slot generally is seen best on satellite photographs.

Dry slot should not be confused with clear slot, which is a storm-scale phenomenon.

Dust Devil A small atmospheric vortex not associated with a thunderstorm, which is made visible by a rotating cloud of dust or debris dust whirl. Dust devils form in response to surface heating during fair, hot weather; they are most frequent in arid or semi-arid regions.

Dust Plume A non-rotating "cloud" of dust raised by straight-line winds. Often seen in a microburst or behind a gust front.

Dust Whirl A rotating column of air rendered visible by dust. Similar to debris; see also *dust devil, gustnado, tornado.*

Dynamics Generally, any forces that produce motion or affect change. In operational meteorology, dynamics usually refer specifically to those forces that produce vertical motion in the atmosphere

E

European Center for Medium-Range Weather Forecasting. ECMWF Operational references in forecast discussions typically refer to the ECMWF's medium-range model. See *MRF, UKMET.*

Electron Avalanche The process in which a relatively small number of free electrons in a gas that is subjected to a strong electric field accelerate, ionize gas atoms by collision, and thus form new electrons to undergo the same process in cumulative fashion. All streamers in a lightning discharge propagate by formation of electron avalanches in regions of high electric field strength that move ahead of their advancing tips. Particularly in the case of the intense return streamer, avalanche processes are enhanced by formation of photoelectrons as a result of ultraviolet radiation emitted by the exited molecules in the region just behind the tip. An avalanche cannot possibly begin until the local electric field strength is high enough to accelerate a free electron to the minimum ionizing speed in the space and time interval corresponding to one mean free path of the electron, for upon collision, the electron usually loses its forward motion in the direction of the field. Maintenance of an avalanche requires a large reservoir of charge, such as accumulates more or less periodically in active thunderstorms.

Electrical Breakdown The sudden decrease of resistivity of a substance when the applied electric field strength rises above a certain threshold value, the substances's electric strength. For air at normal pressures and temperatures, experiment has shown that the breakdown process occurs at a field strength of about 30,000 volts per cm. This value decreases approximately linearly with pressure, and is dependent upon humidity and traces of foreign gases. In the region of high field strength just ahead of an actively growing leader in a lightning stroke, breakdown occurs in the form of a rapidly moving wave of sudden ionization (electron avalanche). The dielectric strength in a cloud of water drops is less than that in cloud-free humid are, for the water drops are distorted as a result of the Macky effect.

Elevated Convection Convection occurring within an elevated layer, i.e., a layer in which the lowest portion is based above the earth's surface. Elevated convection often occurs when air near the ground is relatively cool and stable, e.g., during periods of isentropic lift, when an unstable layer of air is present aloft. In cases of elevated convection, stability indices based on near-surface measurements, such as the lifted index, typically will underestimate the amount of instability present. Severe weather is possible from elevated convection, but is less likely than it is with surface-based convection.

Energy Helicity Index EHI An index that incorporates vertical shear and instability, designed for the purpose of forecasting supercell thunderstorms. It is related directly to storm-relative helicity in the lowest 2 km (SRH, in m2/s2) and CAPE (in j/kg) as follows: EHI= (CAPE x SRH)160,000. Thus, higher values indicate unstable conditions and/or strong vertical shear. Since both parameters are important for severe weather development, higher values generally indicate a greater potential for severe weather. Values of one or more are said to indicate a heightened threat of tornadoes; values of five or more are rarely observed, and are said to indicate potential for violent tornados. However, there are no magic numbers or critical threshold values to confirm or predict the occurrence of tornados of a particular intensity.

Enhanced V A pattern seen on satellite infrared photographs of thunderstorms, in which a thunderstorm anvil exhibits a V-shaped region of cooler cloud tops extending downwind from the thunderstorm core. The enhanced V indicates a very strong updraft, and therefore a higher potential for severe weather. Enhanced V should not be confused with V notch , which is a radar signature.

Enhanced Wording An option used by the SPC in tornado and severe thunderstorm watches when the potential for strong/violent tornados, or unusually widespread damaging straight-line winds, is high. The statement "This is a particularly dangerous situation with the possibility of very damaging tornados" appears in tornado watches with enhanced wording.

Severe thunderstorm watches usually include the statement "This is a particularly dangerous situation with the possibility of extremely damaging winds" when a derecho event is occurring or forecast to occur. See *PDS Watch*

Entrance Region The region upstream from a wind speed maximum in a jet stream (jet max), in which air is approaching (entering) the region of maximum winds, and therefore is accelerating. This acceleration results in a vertical circulation that creates divergence in the upper-level winds in the right half of the entrance region, as would be viewed looking along the direction of flow. This divergence results in upward motion of air in the right rear quadrant, or right entrance region, of the jet max. Severe weather potential sometimes increases in this area as a result. See also *exit region, left exit region.*

Equilibrium Level EL On a sounding, the level above the level of free convection, LFC, at which the temperature of a rising parcel again equals the temperature of the environment.

The height of the EL is the height at which thunderstorm updrafts no longer accelerates upward. Thus, to a close approximation, it represents the height of expected or ongoing thunderstorm tops; however, strong updrafts will continue to rise past the EL before stopping, resulting in storm tops that are higher than the EL. This process sometimes can be seen visually as an overshooting top or anvil dome.

Eta Model One of the operational numerical forecast models run at NCEP. The Eta is run twice daily, with forecast output out to 48 hours.

Exit Region The region downstream from a wind speed maximum in a jet stream (jet max), in which air is moving away from the region of maximum winds, and therefore is decelerating. This deceleration results in divergence in the upper-level winds in the left half of the exit region as would be viewed looking along the direction of flow. This divergence results in upward motion of air in the left front quadrant, or left exit region, of the jet max. Severe weather potential sometimes increases in this area as a result. See also *Entrance Region, Right Entrance Region.*

F

F Scale See *Fujita Scale.*

Feeder Bands Lines or bands of low-level clouds that move (feed) into the updraft region of a thunderstorm, usually from east through south (i.e., parallel to the inflow). Same as inflow bands.

I also use this term in tropical meteorology to describe spiral-shaped bands of convection surrounding, and moving toward, the center of a tropical cyclone.

Fillet Lightning See *Ribbon Lightning.*

Flanking Line A line of cumulus or towering cumulus clouds connected to and extending outward from the most active part of a supercell, usually on the southwest side. The line normally has a stair-step appearance, with the tallest clouds closest to the main storm, and generally coincides with the pseudo-cold front.

Forked Lightning A common form of lightning in a cloud-to-ground discharge which exhibits downward-directed branches from the main lightning channel. This branching is peculiar to the propagation of the stepped leader as it sends out a number of side channels under the influence of the heterogenous space charge in the sub-cloud layer. In general, of the many branches only one is finally established and the other incomplete channels decay after the ascent of the first return.

Forward Flank Downdraft The main region of downdraft in the forward, or leading, part of a supercell, where most of the heavy precipitation is. Compare with *Rear Flank Downdraft*. See *Pseudo-warm Front*.

Front A boundary or transition zone between two air masses of different density and temperature. A moving front is named according to the advancing air mass, e.g., cold front if colder air is advancing.

Fractus Ragged, detached cloud fragments; same as scud.

Fujita Scale or F scale A scale of wind damage intensity in which wind speeds are inferred from an analysis of wind damage.

F0 weak 40-72 mph light damage; F1 weak 73-112 mph moderate damage; F2 strong 113-157 mph considerable damage; F3 strong 158-206 mph severe damage F4; violent 207-260 mph devastating damage F5; violent 261-318 mph (rare) incredible damage. All tornados and most other severe local windstorms are assigned a single number from this scale determined by the most intense damage.

Funnel Cloud A condensation funnel extending from the base of a towering cumulus or CB, associated with a rotating column of air that is not in contact with the ground, hence different from a tornado). A condensation funnel is a tornado, not a funnel cloud, if a) it is in contact with the ground or b) a debris cloud or dust whirl is visible beneath it.

G
Globe Lightning See *ball lightning*

Graupel Also called Snow Pellets, Soft Hail. Precipitation consisting of white, opaque, approximately round, sometimes conical, ice particles 2 to 5 mm in diameter, with a snow-like structure. Graupel is crisp and easily crushed, differing in this respect from snow grains. They rebound when they fall on a hard surface and often break apart.

Ground Clutter A pattern of radar echos from fixed ground targets such as buildings, hills, etc. near the radar. Ground clutter may hide or confuse precipitation echoes near the radar antenna.

Gunge [slang] Anything in the atmosphere that restricts visibility for storm spotting, such as fog, haze, steady rain or drizzle, widespread low clouds (stratus), etc.

Gust Front The leading edge of gusty surface winds from thunderstorm downdrafts; sometimes associated with a shelf cloud or roll cloud. See also *downburst, gustnado, outflow boundary.*

Gustnado or Gustinado [slang] Gust Front Tornado A small tornado, usually weak and short-lived that occurs along the gust front of a thunderstorm. Often it is visible only as a debris cloud or dust whirl near the ground. Gustnados are not associated with storm-scale rotation i.e., mesocyclones; they are more likely to be associated visually with a shelf cloud than with a wall cloud.

H

Heat Lightning Non-technically, the luminosity observed from ordinary lighting too far away for its thunder to be heard. Since such observations have often been made with clear skies overhead, and since hot summer evenings particularly favor this type of observation, a popular but false misconception has it that the presence of diffuse flashes in the apparent absence of thunderclouds implies lightning is somehow occurring in the atmosphere merely as a result of excessive heat.

Helicity A property of a moving fluid which represents the potential for helical flow, flow which follows the pattern of a corkscrew, to evolve. Helicty is proportional to the strength of the flow, the amount of vertical wind shear and the amount of turn in the flow i.e., vorticity. Atmospheric helicty is computed from the vertical wind profile in the lower part of the atmosphere, usually from the surface up to 3 km, and is measured relative to storm motion. Higher values of helicity, generally, around 150 m2/s2 or more, favor the development of mid-level rotation (i.e., mesocyclones). Extreme values can exceed 600 m2/s2.

High Risk (of severe thunderstorms Severe weather is expected to affect more than ten percent of an area. A high risk is rare, and implies an unusually dangerous situation and usually the possibility of a major severe weather outbreak. (see *Slight Risk, Moderate Risk, Convective Outlook*).

Hodograph A plot representing the vertical distribution of horizontal winds, using polar coordinates. A hodograph is obtained by plotting the end points of the wind vectors at various altitudes, and connecting these points in order of increasing height. Interpretation of a hodograph can help in forecasting the subsequent evolution of thunderstorms, e.g., squall line vs. supercells, splitting vs. non-splitting storms, tornadic vs. nontornadic storms, etc.

Hook or Hook Echo A radar reflectivity pattern characterized by a hook-shaped extension of a thunderstorm echo, usually in the right-rear part of the storm (relative to its direction of motion). A hook often is associated with mesocyclone, and indicates favorable conditions for tornado development.

HP Storm also called HP Supercell-High-Precipitation Storm or High-Precipitation supercell A supercell thunderstorm in which heavy precipitation, including hail, falls on the trailing side of the mesocyclone. Precipitation often totally envelops the region of rotation, making visual identification of any embedded tornados difficult and very dangerous. Unlike most classic supercells, the region of rotation in many HP storms develops in the front-flank region of the storm usually in the eastern portion. HP storms often produce extreme and prolonged downburst events, serious flash flooding, and very large damaging hail events. Mobile storm spotter are strongly advised to maintain a safe distance from any storm that has been identified as an HP storm, close observations (e.g., core punching) can be extremely dangerous. See *Bear's Cage.*

Humidity Generally, a measure of the water vapor content of the air. Popularly, it is used synonymously with relative humidity.

I

Impulse See *upper level system*

Inflow bands also called Feeder Bands Bands of low clouds, arranged parallel to the low-level winds and moving into or toward a thunderstorm. They may indicate the strength of the inflow of moist air into the storm, and, hence, its potential severity. Spotters should be especially wary of inflow bands that curve in a manner suggesting cyclonic rotation.

Inflow Jets Local jets of air near the ground flowing inward toward the base of a tornado.

Inflow Notch A radar signature characterized by an indentation in the reflectivity pattern on the inflow side of the storm. The indentation is often I V-shaped, but this term should not be confused with the V-notch. Supercell thunderstorms often exhibit inflow notches, usually in the right quadrant of a classic supercell, but sometimes in the eastern part of an HP storm or in the rear part of a storm (rear inflow notch).

Inflow Stinger A beaver tail cloud with a stinger-like shape.

Insolation Incoming solar radiation. Solar heating; sunshine.

Instability The tendency for air parcels to accelerate when they are displaced from their original positions, especially, the tendency to acclerate upward after being lifted. Instability is a prerequisite for severe weather; the greater the instability, the greater the potential for severe thunderstorms. See *Lifted Index*.

Inversion Generally, a departure from the usual increase or decrease in an atmospheric property with altitude. Specifically, it almost always refers to a temperature inversion, i.e., an increase in temperature with height, or to the layer within which such an increase occurs. An inversion is present in the lower part of a cap.

Isentropic Lift Lifting of air that is traveling along an upward- sloping,isentropic surface. Isentropic lift often is referred to erroneously as over running, but more accurately describes the physical process by which the lifting occurs. Siuations involving isentropic lift often are characterized by widespread stratiform clouds and precipitation, but may include elevated convection in the form of embedded thunderstorms.

Isentropic Surface A two-dimensional surface containing points of equal potential temperature.

Isobar A line connecting points of equal pressure.

Isodrosotherm A line connecting points of equal dew point temperature.

Isohyet A line connecting points of equal precipitation amounts.

Isopleth General term for a line connecting points of equal value of some quantity. Isobars, isotherms, etc., all are examples of isopleths.

Isotach A line connecting points of equal wind speed.

Isotherm A line connecting points of equal temperature.

J

Jet Max or Speed Max or Jet Streak A point or area of relative maximum wind speeds within a jet stream.

Jet Streak A local wind speed maximum with a jet stream.

Jet Stream Relatively strong winds concentrated in a narrow stream in the atmosphere , normally referring to horizontal, high-altitude winds. The position and orientation of jet streams vary from day to day. General weather patterns—(hot/cold, wet, dry—are related closely to the position, strength, and orientation of the jet stream(s). A jet steam at low levels is known as a low-level jet.

K

Knuckles [slang] Lumpy protrusions on the edges, and sometimes the underside, of a thunderstorm anvil. They usually appear on the upwind side of a back-sheared anvil, and indicate rapid expansion of the anvil due to the presence of a very strong updraft. They are not mammatus clouds. See also *Cumuliform Anvil, Anvil Rollover.*

L

Laminar Smooth, non-turbulent. Often used to describe cloud formations which appear to be shaped by a smooth flow of air traveling in parallel layers or sheets.

Landspout [slang] A tornado that does not arise from organized storm- scale rotation and therefore is not associated with a wall cloud, visually, or mesocyclone, on radar. Landspouts typically are observed beneath Cbs or towering cumulus clouds, often as no more than a dust whirl, and essentially are the land-based equivalents of Lapse Rate, the rate of change of an atmospheric variable, usually temperature, with height. A steep lapse rate implies a rapid decrease in temperature with height, a sign of instability, and a steepening lapse rate implies that destabilization is occurring.

Large-Scale See *Synoptic-Scale*

Leader The streamer which initiates the first phase of each stroke of a lightning discharge. Like all streamers, it is a channel of very high ion density which propagates through the air by the continual establishment of an electron avalanche ahead of its tip. Of the recognized types of leader, the stepped leader initiates the very first stroke and establishes the channel for all subsequent streamers of a lightning discharge. The dart leader initiates each subsequent stroke.

Left Front Quadrant or Left Exit Region Looking along the direction of flow the area downstream from and to the left of an upper-level jet max. Upward motion and severe thunderstorm potential sometimes is increased in this area relative to the wind speed maximum. See also *Entrance Region, Right Rear Quadrant.*

Left Mover A thunderstorm which moves to the left relative to the steering winds and to other nearby thunderstorms, often the northern part of a splitting storm. See also *Right Mover.*

Line Echo Wave Pattern LEWP A bulge in a thunderstorm line producing a wave-shaped "kink" in the line. The potential for strong outflow and damaging straight-line winds increases near the bulge, which often resembles a bow echo. Severe weather potential also is increased with storms near the crest of a LEWP.

Lifted Index LI A common measure of atmospheric instability. Its value is obtained by computing the temperature that air near the ground would have if it were lifted to some higher level usually 18,000 feet and comparing that temperature to the actual temperature at the level. Negative values indicate instability. The more negative, the more instable the air is and the stronger the updrafts are likely to be with any developing thunderstorms. However, there are no "magic" numbers or threshold LI values below which severe weather becomes imminent.

Loaded Gun Sounding [slang] An instability containing a cap, explosive thunderstorm development can be expected if the cap can be weakened or the air below is heated sufficiently to overcome it.

Longwave Trough A trough in the prevailing westerly flow aloft which is characterized by large length and long duration. Generally, there are no more than five longwave troughs around the Northern Hemisphere at any given time. Their position and intensity govern general weather patterns (e.g., hot/cold, wet/dry) over periods of days, weeks, or months. Smaller disturbances, such asshortwave troughs, typically move more rapidly through the broader flow of a longwave trough, producing weather changes over shorter time periods, a day or less. The term also may be used to describe a narrow zone of strong winds above the boundary layer, but in this sense the more proper term would be low-level jet stream.

LP Storm or LP Supercell, Low-Precipitation Storm or Low-Precipitation Supercell A supercell thunderstorm characterized by a relative lack of visible precipitation. Visually similar to a classic supercell, except without the heavy pecipitation core. LP storms often exhibit a striking visual appearance; the main tower often is bell-shaped, with a corkscrew appearance suggesting rotation. They are capable of producing tornados and very large hail. Radar identification often is difficult relative to other types of supercells, so visual reports are very important. LP storms almost always occur on or near the dry line, and thus are sometimes referred to as dry line storms.

LSR- Local Storm Report LSR A product issued by local NWS offices to inform readers of severe and significant weather-related events.

M

Main Stoke See *return streamer.*

Mammatus Clouds *Rounded, smooth, sack-like protrusions hanging from the underside of a cloud, usually a thunderstorm anvil. Mammatus clouds often accompany severe thunderstorms, but do not produce severe weather; they may accompany non-severe storms as well.*

Mesoscale Convective Complex MCC Generally round or oval-shaped, which normally reaches peak intensity at night. The formal definition includes specific minimum criteria for size, duration, and eccentricity, i.e., "roundness", based on the cloud shield as seen on infrared satellite photographs.

Size: Area of cloud top -32 degree C or less: 100,00 square kilometers or more (slightly smaller than the

state of Ohio), and area of cloud top -52 degrees C
or less: 50,000 square kilometers or more
Duration: Size criteria must be met for at least 6
hours
Eccentricity: Minor/major axis at least 0.7.
MCC's typically form during the afternoon and evening in the form of several isolated thunderstorms,
during which time the potential for severe weather
is greatest. During peak intensity, the primary threat
shifts toward heavy rain and flooding.

Mesoscale Convective System MCSA complex of thunderstorms which becomes organized on a scale larger
than the individual thunderstorms, and normally
persists for several hours or more. MCS's may be
round or linear in shape, and include systems such
as tropical cyclones and squall lines

Medium Range In forecasting, generally three days in advance.

Meridional Flow Large-scale atmospheric flow in which
the north-south component (i.e., longitudinal, or
along a meridian) is pronounced. The accompanying
zonal east-west component is often weaker than normal. Compare with *Zonal Flow*.

Mesocyclone A storm-scale region of rotation, typically
two to six miles in diameter and often found in the
right rear flank of a supercell or on the eastern, or
front, flank of an HP storm. The circulation of a mesocyclone covers an area much larger than the tornado that may develop within it.

Properly used, mesocyclone is a radar term; it is
defined as a rotation signature appearing on Doppler
radar that meets specific criteria for magnitude, vertical depth, and duration. Therefore, a mesocyclone
should not be considered a visually-observable phenomenon, although visual evidence of rotation, such

as curved inflow bands, may imply the presence of a mesocyclone.

Mesohigh A mesoscale high pressure area, usually associated with MCS's or their remnants.

Mesolow or Sub-Synoptic Low A mesoscale low-pressure center. Severe weather potential often increases in the area near and just ahead of a mesolow. Mesolow should not be confused with mesocyclone, which is a storm-scale phenomenon.

Mesonet A regional network of observing surface stations designed to diagnose mesoscale weather features and their associated processes.

Mesoscale Size scale referring to weather systems smaller than synoptic- scale systems but larger than storm-scale systems. Horizontal dimensions generally range from around fifty miles to several hundred miles. Squall lines, MCC's, and MCS's, are examples of mesoscale weather systems.

Microburst A small, concentrated downburst affecting an area less than four kilometers across. Most are rather short-lived, (five minutes or so, but on rare occasions they have been known to last up to six times that long. Microbursts can produce winds a s high as 146 knots.

Mid-Level Cooling Local cooling of the air in the middle levels of the atmosphere roughly 8 to 25 thousand feet, which can lead to destablization of the entire atmosphere if all other factors are squall. Mid-level cooling can occur, for example with the approach of amid-level cold pool.

Moderate Risk (of severe thunderstorms) Severe thunderstorms are expected to affect between five and ten percent of the area. A moderate risk indicates the possibility of a significant severe weather episode. See *High Risk, Slight Risk, Convective Outlook.*

Moisture Advection Transport of moisture by horizontal winds.

Moisture Convergence A measure of the degree to which moist air is converging into a given area, taking into account the effect of converging winds and moisture advection. Areas of persistent moisture convergence are favored regions for thunderstorm development, if other factors, such as instability, are favorable.

Morning Glory An elongated cloud band, visually similar to a roll cloud, usually appearing in the morning hours when the atmosphere is relatively stable. Morning glories result from perturbations related to gravitational waves in a stable boundary layer. They are similar to ripples on a water surface; several parallel morning glories often can be seen propagating in the same direction.

Medium Range Forecast MRF Model One of the operational forecast models run at NCEP. The MRF is run once daily, with forecast output out to 240 hours (10 days).

Multi-cell Thunderstorm A thunderstorm consisting of two or more cells, of which most or all are often visible at a given time as distinct domes or towers in various stages of development.

Nearly all thunderstorms, including supercells, are multi-cellular, but the term is often used to describe a storm which does not fit the definition of a supercell.

Multiple-Vortex or Multi-Vortex Tornado A tornado in which two or more condensation funnels or debris clouds are present at the same time, often rotating about a common center or about each other. Multiple-vortex tornadoes can be especially damaging. See *Suction Vortex*.

Mushroom [slang] A thunderstorm with a well-defined anvil rollover, that resembles a mushroom.

N

National Centers for Environmental Prediction NCEP The modernized version of NMC.

Negative-Tilt Trough An upper level system which is tilted to the west with increasing latitude, i.e., with an axis from southeast to northwest. A negative-tilt trough often is a sign of a developing or intensifying system.

Newton A unit of force equal to 1kg/m s2.

NEXt-Generation Weather RADar NEXRAD Technologically-advanced weather radar being deployed to replace WSR-57 and WSR-74 units. NEXRAD is a high-resolution Doppler radar with increased emphasis on automation, including use of algorithms and automated volume scans. NEXRAD units are known as WSR-88D.

Nested Grid Model NGM One of the operational forecast models run at NCEP. The NGM is run twice daily, with forecast output out to 48 hours.

National Meteorological Center NMC with headquarters near Washington D.C.; now known as NCEP.

National Oceanographic and Atmospheric Administration NOAA.

NOAA Weather Radio A service of NOAA and the U.S. Department of Commerce, designed to speed warnings of natural disasters and national emergencies to the general public and emergency action units. NOAA Weather Radio broadcasts are made from National Weather Service offices 24 hours a day. Taped weather forecast messages are repeated every 4 to 6 minutes and are routinely revised every 2 to 3 hours, or more frequently if needed. During emergency situations, NWS can interrupt the routine weather broadcast and substitute special warning messages. They can also activate specially designated warning receivers. These receivers will either sound an alarm indicating that an emergency exists and the listener should tune-in frequently or, when operated in muted mode, will be automatically turned on so the warning message can be heard.

Nocturnal Relating to nighttime, or occurring at night.

Nowcast A short-term weather forecast, generally out to six hours or less.

National Severe Storms Forecast Center NSSFC in Kansas City MO; now known as SPC.

National Severe Storms Laboratory NSSL in Norman OK. Sometimes pronounced NEES-sel.

Numerical Weather Predication NWP

National Weather Service NS

O

Occluded Mesocyclone A mesocyclone in which air from the rear-flank downdraft has completely enveloped the circulation at low levels, cutting of the inflow of warm unstable low-level air.

Orographic Related to, or caused by, physical geography, such as mountains or sloping terrain.

Orographic Lift Lifting of air caused by its passage up and over mountains or other sloping terrain.

Orphan Anvil [slang] An anvil from a dissipated thunderstorm, below which no other clouds remain.

Outflow Boundary A mesoscale boundary separating thunderstorm-cooled air (outflow) from the surrounding air; similar in effect to a cold front, with passage marked by a wind shift and usually a drop in temperature. Outflow boundaries may persist for

24 hours or more after the thunderstorms that generated them dissipate, and may travel hundreds of miles from their area of origin. New thunderstorms often develop along outflow boundaries, especially near the point of intersection with another boundary—cold front, dry line, another outflow boundary, etc. See *triple point*.

Overhang Radar term indicating a region of high reflectivity at middle and upper levels above an area of weak reflectivity at low levels. The latter area is known as a weak-echo region, or WER. The overhang is found on the inflow side of a thunderstorm, normally the south or southeast side.

Overrunning A weather pattern in which a relatively warm air mass is in motion above another air mass of greater density at the surface. Embedded thunderstorms sometimes develop in such a pattern; severe thunderstorms with large hail can occur, but tornadoes are unlikely.

Overrunning is often applied to the case of warm air riding up over a retreating layer of colder air, as along the sloping surface of a warm front. Such use of the term technically is incorrect, but in general it refers to a pattern characterized by widespread clouds and steady precipitation on the cool side of the front or other boundary.

Overshooting Top or Penetrating Top A dome-like protrusion above a thunderstorm anvil, representing a very strong updraft and hence a higher potential for severe weather. A persistent and/or large overshooting top, anvil dome is present on a supercell. A short-lived overshooting top, or one that forms and dissipates in cycles, may indicate the presence of a pulse storm or a cyclic storm.

P

Pearl Lightning Same as beaded lightning

PDS Watch [slang] A tornado watch with enhanced wording—Particularly Dangerous Situation

Pendant Echo Radar signature generally similar to a hook echo, except that the hook shape is not as well defined.

Penetrating Top same as overshooting top.

Popcorn Convection [slang] Showers and thunderstorms that form on a scattered basis with little or no apparent organization, usually during the afternoon in response to diurnal heating. Individual thunderstorms are typically the type sometimes referred to as air mass thunderstorms; small, short -lived, very rarely severe, which almost always dissipate near or just after sunset.

Positive Area The area on a sounding representing the layer in which a lifted parcel would be warmer than the environment; thus, the area between the environmental temperature profile and the path of the lifted parcel. Positive area is a measure of the energy available for convection. See *CAPE*.

Positive CG A CG flash that delivers positive charge to the ground, as opposed to the more common negative charge. Positive CG's occur more frequently in some severe thunderstorms. They can be detected by most lightning detection networks, but visually it is impossible to distinguish between a positive CG and a negative CG. Some people have claimed to observe a relationship between staccato lightning and positive CG's, but this relationship is as yet unproven.

Positive-Tilt Trough An upper level system which is tilted to the east with increasing latitude, i.e., from southwest to northeast. A positive-tilt trough is often a sign of a weakening weather system, and generally is less likely to result in severe weather than a nega-tive-tilt trough if all other factors are equal.

Potential Temperature The temperature a parcel of dry air would have if brought adiabatically, that is with-out transfer of heat or mass, to a standard pressure level of 1000mb.

Plan Position Indicates No Echoes PPINE refers to the fact that a radar detects no precipitation within its range.

Profiler An instrument designed to measure horizontal winds directly above its location, and thus measure the vertical wind profile. Profilers operate on the same principles as Doppler Radar.

Pseudo-Cold Front A boundary between a supercell's in-flow region and the rear-flank downdraft or RFD. It extends outward from the mesocyclone center, usu-ally toward the south or southwest but may bow out-ward to the east or southeast in the case of an occluded mesocyclone, and is characterized by the downdraft air advancing toward the inflow region. It is a particular form of gust front. See also *pseudo-warm front.*

Pulse Storm A thunderstorm within which a brief period or pulse may produce a strong tornado but often pro-duces large hail and/or damaging winds. See *over-shooting top, cyclic storm.*

Positive Vorticity Advection PVA Advection of higher values of vorticity into an area, which is often associ-ated with upward motion (lifting) of the air. PVA typically is found in advance of disturbances aloft, shortwaves, and is a property which often enhances the potential for thunderstorm development.

R

RAdar DAta Processor II RADAP II Attached to some WSR-57 and WSR- 74 radar units, it automatically controls the tilt sequence and computes several radar-derived quantities at regular intervals, including VIL, storm tops, accumulated rainfall, etc.

Relative Humidity The ratio, expressed as a percent, of the actual amount of moisture content in vapor form in a volume of air to the amount that would be present if the air were saturated . Since the saturation amount is dependent on temperature, relative humidity is a function of both moisture content and temperature. As such, relative humidity by itself does not directly indicate the actual amount of atmospheric moisture present. See *Dew Point.*

Retrogression or Retrograde Motion Movement of a weather system in a direction opposite to that of the basic flow in which it is embedded, usually referring to a closed low or a longwave trough which moves westward.

Return Streamer also called a Return Stroke or Main Stroke The intensely luminous streamer which propagates upward from the earth to cloud base in the last phase of each lightning stroke of a cloud-to-ground discharge. In a typical composite flash, the first return streamer ascends as soon as the descending stepped leader makes electrical contact with the earth, often aided by short ascending ground streamers. The second and all subsequent return streamers differ only in that they are initiated by a dart leader and not a stepped leader. It is the return streamer which yields almost all of the luminosity and charge transfer in most cloud-to-ground strokes. Its great speed of ascent—3x10 7 m/s, about 1/10 the speed of light—is made possible by the residual ionization of the lightning channel remaining from the passage of the immediately preceding leader, and this charge is enhanced by the convergent nature of the electrical field in which channel electrons are drawn down toward the ascending tip in the region of the streamer's electron avalanche. Current peaks as high as 165,000 amperes have been reported, and values of 20,000 amperes are typical. The return streamer's current wave ends when the available charge center within the cloud has been depopulated of mobile ions. The entire process of return streamer action is completed in a few tens of microseconds, and most of this time is spent in a long decay period following an early rapid rise to full current in only a few microseconds. The return streamer of close-to-ground discharges is so intense because of the high electrical conductivity of the ground and hence this type of streamer is not found in air discharges, cloud discharges, or cloud-to-cloud discharges.

Return Flow South winds on the back or west side of an eastward-moving surface high pressure system, Return flow over the central and eastern United States typically results in a return of moist from the Gulf of Mexico or Atlantic Ocean.

Ribbon Lightning also called Band Lightning or Fillet Lightning Ordinary streak lightning that appears to spread horizontally into a ribbon of parallel luminous streaks when a very strong wind is blowing at right angles to the observer's line of sight. Successive strokes of the lightning flash are then displaced by small angular amounts and may appear to the eye or camera as distinct paths. The same effect is readily created artificially by the rapid transverse movement of a camera during film exposure.

Right Entrance Region or Right Rear Quadrant The area upstream from and to the right of an upper-level jet max, as would be seen looking along the direction of flow. Upward motion and severe thunderstorm potential sometimes are increased in this area relative to the wind speed maximum. See also *Exit Region, Left Front Quadrant.*

Ridge An elongated area of relatively high atmospheric pressure; the opposite of trough.

Right Mover A thunderstorm that moves appreciably to tho right relative to the main steering winds and to other nearby thunderstorms. Right movers typically are associated with a high potential for severe weather. Supercells often are right movers. See *Left Mover, Splitting Storm.*

Right Rear Quadrant See *Right Entrance Region*

Rocket Lightning A rare form of lightning whose luminous channel seems to advance through the air with the speed of a rocket. The slow speed of such discharges is presumably due to low ion concentration in the air being invaded by the channel and to low electric field strengths at the tip of the leader. This is not a fully satisfactory explanation because even the minimum ionizing speed of a free electron is actually very great, and it is not clear how any leader propagates at a speed much below this. Rocket lightning, like ball lightning, must still be regarded as an interesting mystery of thunderstorm electricity.

Roll Cloud A low, horizontal tube-shaped arcus cloud associated with a thunderstorm gust front or sometimes with a cold front. Roll clouds are relatively rare; they are completely detached from the thunderstorm base or other cloud features, thus differentiating them from the more familiar shelf clouds. Roll clouds usually appear to be "rolling" about the horizontal axis, but should not be confused with funnel clouds.

Rope or Rope Funnel A narrow, often contorted condensation funnel usually associated with the decaying stage of a tornado. See **Rope Stage**

Rope Cloud In satellite meteorology, a narrow, rope-like band of clouds sometimes seen on satellite images along a front or other boundary. The term is sometimes used synonymously with rope or rope funnel.

Rope Stage The dissipating stage of a tornado, characterized by the thinning and shrinking of the condensation funnel into a rope or rope funnel. Damage is possible during this stage.

Rapid Update Cycle RUC A numerical model run at NCEP that focuses on short-term—up to 12 hour—forecasts and small-scale, mesoscale, weather features. Forecast are prepared every three hours.

S

Scud or Fractus Small, ragged, low cloud fragments that are unattached to a larger cloud base and often seen with and behind cold fronts and thunderstorm gust fronts. Such clouds generally are associated with cool moist air, such as thunderstorm outflow.

SEvere Local Storms Unit SELS Former name of the Operations Branch of the Storm Predication Center (SPC) in Norman, Olahoma, formerly in Kansas City, MO.

Severe Thunderstorm A thunderstorm which produces tornadoes, hail 0.75 inches or more in diameter, or winds of 50 knots or more. Structural wind damage may imply the occurrence of a severe thunderstorm. See *Approaching (severe).*

Shear Variation in wind speed (speed shear) and/or direction (directional shear) over a short distance. Shear usually refers to vertical wind shear, the change in wind with height; however, the term also is used in Doppler Radar to describe changes in radial velocity over short horizontal distances.

Sheet Lightning Also called Luminous Cloud. A diffuse, but sometimes fairly bright, illumination of those parts of a thundercloud that surround the path of a lighting flash, particularly a cloud discharge manifestation; or ordinary lightning types in the presence of obscuring clouds.

Shelf Cloud A low, horizontal wedge-shaped arcus cloud, associated with a thunderstorm gust front, or occasionally with a cold front, even in the absence of thunderstorms. Unlike the roll cloud, the shelf cloud is attached to the base of the parent cloud above it, usually a thunderstorm. Rising cloud motion can often be seen in the leading, outer, part of the shelf cloud, while the underside usually appears turbulent, boiling, and wind-torn.

Short-Fuse Warning A warning issued by the NWS for a local weather hazard of relatively short duration. Short-fuse warnings include tornado warnings, severe thunderstorm warnings, and flash flood warnings. Tornado and severe thunder storm warnings typically are issued for periods of an hour or less, flash flood warnings typically for three hours or less.

Shortwave or Shortwave Trough A disturbance in the mid or upper part of the atmosphere which induces upward motion ahead of it. If other conditions are favorable, the upward motion can contribute to thunderstorm development ahead of a shortwave.

Slight Risk (of severe thunderstorms) Severe thunderstorms are expected to affect between two and five percent of an area. A slight risk generally implies that severe weather events are expect to be isolated. See *High Risk, Moderate Risk, Convective Outlook.*

Sounding A plot of the vertical profile of temperature and dew point, and often winds above a fixed location. Soundings are used extensively in severe weather forecasting, e.g., to determine instability, locate temperature inversions, measure the strength of the cap, obtain the convective temperature, etc.

Storm Predication Center SPC A national forecast center in Norman, Oklahoma, which is part of the NCEP. The SPC is responsible for providing short-term forecast guidance for severe convection, excessive rainfall, flash flooding and severe winter weather over the contiguous United States.

Speed Shear The component of wind shear which is due to a change in wind speed with height, e.g., southwesterly winds of 20 mph at 10,000 feet increasing to 50 mph at 20,000 feet. Speed shear is an important factor in severe weather development, especially in the middle and upper levels of the atmosphere.

Spin-up [slang] A small-scale vortex initiation, may be seen when a gustnado, land spout, or suction vortex forms.

Splitting Storm A thunderstorm which splits into two storms which follow diverging paths: a left mover and a right mover. The left mover typically moves faster than the original storm, the right mover, more slowly. Of the two, the left mover is most likely to weaken and dissipate although on rare occasions it can become a very severe anticyclonic-rotating storm, while the right mover is the one most likely to reach supercell status.

Sprite Massive but weak luminous flashes that appear directly above an active thunderstorm system and are coincident with cloud-to-ground or intracloud lightning strokes. Their spatial structures range from small single or multiple vertically elongated spots, to spots with faint extrusions above and below, to bright groupings which extend from the cloud tops to altitudes of 95 km. Sprites are predominantly red.

The brightest region lies in the altitude range 65-75 km, above which there is often a faint red glow or wispy structure that extends to about 90 km. Below the bright red region, blue tendril-like filamentary structures often extend downward to a low of 40 km. Sprites rarely appear singly, usually occurring in clusters of two, three, or more. Some of the very large events seem to be tightly packed clusters of many individual sprites. Other events are more loosely packed and may extend across horizontal distances of 50 km or more and occupy atmospheric volumes it excess of 10,000 cubic km.

High speed photometer measurements show that the duration of sprites is only a few ms. Current evidence strongly suggests that sprites usually occur in decaying portions of thunderstorms and are correlated with large positive cloud-to-ground lightning strokes. The optical intensity of sprite clusters, estimated by comparison with tabulated stellar intensities, is comparable to a moderately bright auroral arc. The optical energy is roughly 10-50 kj per event, with a corresponding optical power of 5-25 MW. Assuming that optical energy constitutes 1/1000 of the total for the event, the energy and power are on the order of 10-100 MJ and 5-50 GW, respectively.

If sprites are only barely detectable by the un-aided human eye, in intensified television images obtained from the ground and from aircraft show then as dazzlingly complex structures that assume a variety of forms.

Early research reports for these events referred to them by a variety of names, including "upward lightning," "upward discharges," cloud-to-stratosphere discharges," and "cloud-to-ionosphere discharges." Now they are simply referred to as sprites, a whimsical term that evokes a sense of their fleeting nature, while at the same time remaining nonjudgemental about physical processes that have yet to be determined. See also *Blue Jets.*

Squall Line A solid or nearly solid line or band of active thunderstorms.

Stable Air is stable if, when forced to move either upward or downward it will return to its original level when the forcing is released.

Staccato Lightning A CG lightning discharge which appears as a single very bright, short-duration stroke, often with considerable branching.

Steering Winds or Steering Currents A prevailing synoptic scale flow which governs the movement of smaller features embedded within it.

Stellar Lightning Lightning consisting of several flashes that seem to radiate from a single point.

St. Elmo's Fire also called Corposant. This name was given the phenomenon by Mediterranean sailors who regarded it as a visitation of their patron saint, St. Elmo (Erasmus). An appearance of St. Elmo's fire was regarded as a good omen, for it tends to occur in the last phases of a violent thunderstorm when most of the surface wind and wave disturbance is over. See *Corona Discharge.*

Stepped Leader The initial streamer of a lightning discharge, and intermittently advancing column of high ion-density which establish the channel for subsequent return streamers and dart leaders. The peculiar characteristic of this type of leader is its step-wise growth at intervals of about fifty to one hundred microseconds. The velocity of growth during the brief intervals of advance, each only about one microsecond in duration, is quite high (about 5x10 to the ninth power cm/s), but the long stationary phases reduce its effective speed to only about 5x10 to the seventh power cm/s (roughly 1/1000th the speed of light). Stepped leaders typically exhibit some degree of branching because they tend to grow in an exploratory manner, seeking the optimal path through the air.

Storm-Relative Measure relative to a moving thunderstorm, usually referring to winds, wind shear, or helicity.

Storm-Scale Refers to weather systems with sizes on the order of individual thunderstorms. See *Synoptic-Scale, Mesoscale.*

Straight-Line Winds Generally, any winds that are not associated with rotation, used mainly to differentiate them from torndadic winds.

Stratiform Having extensive horizontal development, as opposed to the more vertical development characteristic of convection. Stratiform clouds cover large areas but show relatively little vertical development. Stratiform precipitation, in general, is relatively continuous and uniform in intensity, i.e., steady rain versus rain showers.

Stratocumulus Low-level clouds, existing in a relatively flat layer but having individual elements. Elements are often arranged in rows, bands, or waves. Stratocumulus often reveals the depth of the moist air at low levels, while the speed of the cloud elements can reveal the strength of the low-level jet.

Stratus A low, generally gray cloud layer with a fairly uniform base. Stratus may appear in the form of ragged patches, but otherwise does not exhibit individual cloud elements as do cumulus and stratocumulus clouds. Fog is usually a surface-based form of stratus.

Streamer A sinuous channel of very high ion-density which propagates itself through a gas by continual establishment of an electron avalanche just ahead of its advancing tip. In the lightning discharge, the stepped leader, dart leader, and return streamer, all constitute special types of streamers.

Streak Lighting Ordinary lightning of a cloud-to-ground discharge, that appears to be entirely concentrated in a single, relatively straight lightning channel

Striations Grooves or channels in cloud formations, arranged parallel to the flow of air and therefore depicting the airflow relative to the parent cloud. Striations often reveal the presence of rotation, as in the barber pole or "corkscrew" effect often observed with the rotating updraft of an LP storm.

Subsidence Sinking motion in the atmosphere, usually over a broad area.

Sub-Synoptic Low Essentially the same as mesolow.

Suction Vortex or Suction Spot A small but very intense vortex within a tornado circulation. Several suction vortices typically are present in a multiple vortex tornado. Much of the extreme damage associated with violent tornadoes F4 and F5 on the Futjia scale, is attributed to suction vortices.

Supercell A thunderstorm with a persistent rotating updraft. Supercells are rare, but are responsible for a remarkably high percentage of severe weather events—especially tornadoes, extremely large hail and damaging straight-line winds. Being right movers they frequently travel to the right of the main environmental winds. Radar characteristics often, but not always, include a hook or pendant, bounded weak echo region (BWER), V-notch, mesocyclone, and sometimes a TVS. Visual characteristics often include a rain-free base (with or without a wall cloud), tail cloud, flanking line, overshooting top, and back-sheared anvil, all of which are normally observed in or near the right rear or southwest part of the storm. Storms exhibiting these characteristics may be called classic supercells; however, HP storms and LP storms also are supercell varieties.

Surface Based Convection Convection occurring within a surface-based layer, i.e., a layer in which the lowest potion is based at or very near the earth's surface. Compare with *Elevated Convection.*

Severe Weather ThrEAT Index SWEAT Index A stablility index developed by the Air Force which incorporates instablility, wind shear, and wind speed. SWEAT values of about 250-300 or more indicate a greater potential for severe weather, but as with all stability indices, there are no magic numbers.

SWADY1, SWODY2 Day-1 and Day-2 convective outlooks issued by SELS.

Synoptic Scale or Large Scale Size scale referring generally to weather systems with horizontal dimensions of several hundred miles or more. Most high and low pressure areas seen on weather maps are synoptic-scale systems. Compare with *Mesocscale, Storm-Scale.*

T

Tail Cloud A horizontal, tail shaped cloud at low levels extending from the precipitation cascade region of a supercell toward the wall cloud, usually observed extending from the wall cloud toward the north or northeast. The base of the tail cloud is about the same as that of the wall cloud. Cloud motion in the tail cloud is away from the precipitation and toward the wall cloud, with rapid upward motion often observed near the junction of the tail and wall clouds.

See *Supercell.*

Compare with beaver tail, which is a form of inflow band that normally attaches to the storm's main updraft, not to the wall cloud, and has a base at about the same level as the updraft base, not the wall cloud.

Tail-End Charlie [slang] The thunderstorm at the southernmost end of a squall line or other line or band of thunderstorms. Since low-level southerly inflow of warm, moist air into this storm is relatively unimpeded, such a storm often has a higher probability of strengthening to severe levels than the other storms in the line.

Thermodynamic Chart or Thermodynamic Diagram A chart containing contours of pressure, temperature, moisture, and potential temperature, all drawn relative to each other to satisfy basic thermodynamic laws. Such a chart typically is used to plot atmospheric sounds and to estimate potential changes in temperature, moisture, etc., if air were displaced vertically from a given level. A thermodynamic chart is a useful tool in diagnosing atmospheric instability.

Thermoelectric Effect The process whereby a temperature gradient in ice crystals produces a separation of electrical charges with positive charges in the colder portions.

Theta-e (or Equivalent Potential Temperature) The temperature a parcel of air would have if a) it was lifted until it became saturated, b) all water vapor was condensed out, and c) it was returned without transfer of heat or mass) to a pressure of 1000 millibars. Theta-e, which typically is expressed in degrees Kelvin, is directly related to the amount of heat present in an air parcel. It is useful in diagnosing atmospheric instability.

Theta-e Ridge An axis of relatively high values of theta-e. Severe weather and excessive rainfall often occur near or just upstream from a theta-e ridge.

Thunderbolt In mythology, a lightning flash accompanied by a material "bolt" or "dart." The legendary cause of the damage done by lightning. It is still used as a lightning discharge accompanied by thunder.

Tilt Sequence Radar term indicating that the radar antenna is scanning through a series of antenna elevations to obtain a volume scan.

Tilted Storm- or Tilted Updraft A thunderstorm or cloud tower which is not purely vertical but instead exhibits a slanted or titled character. It is a sign of vertical wind shear, a favorable condition for severe storm development.

Tornado A violently rotating column of air in contact with the ground and extending from the base of a thunderstorm. A condensation funnel does not need to reach to the ground for a tornado to be present. A debris cloud beneath a thunderstorm is all that is needed to confirm the presence of a tornado, even in the total absence of a condensation funnel.

Tornado Family A series of tornadoes produced by a single supercell, resulting in damage path segments along the same general line.

Total-Totals Index A stability index and severe weather forecast tool, equal to the temperature at 850 mb plus the dew point at 850 mb, minus twice the temperature at 500 mb. The total-totals index is the arithmetic sum of two other indices, the Vertical Totals Index (temperature at 850 mb minus temperature at 500 mb) and the Cross Totals Index (dew point at 850 mb minus temperature at 500 mb) As with all stability indices there are no magic threshold values, but in general, values of less than 50 or greater than

55 are considered weak and strong indicators, respectively, of potential severe storm development.

Tower short for towering cumulus A cloud element showing appreciable upward vertical development.

Towering Cumulus Congestus A large cumulus cloud with great vertical development, usually with a cauliflower-like appearance, but lacking the characteristics anvil of a Cb.

Transverse Bands Bands of clouds that are perpendicular to the flow in which they are embedded. They are often seen best on satellite photographs. Seen at high levels, they may indicate severe or extreme turbulence. Transverse bands called transverse rolls or T rolls seen at low levels often indicate the presence of a temperature inversion or cap as well as directional shear in the low-to-mid level winds. These conditions usually favor the development of strong to severe thunderstorms.

Transverse Rolls Elongated low-level clouds, arranged in parallel bands and aligned parallel to the low-level winds, but perpendicular to the mid-level flow. Transverse rolls are one type of transverse band, and often indicate an environment favorable for the subsequent development of supercells. Since they are aligned parallel to the low-level inflow, they may point toward the region most likely for later storm development.

T-Rolls [slang] same as transverse rolls.

Triple Point The intersection point between two boundaries—dryline, outflow boundary, cold front, etc.—often a focus for thunderstorm development.

Triple point may also refer to a point on the gust front of a supercell, where the warm moist inflow, the rain-cooled outflow from the forward flank downdraft, and the rear flank downdraft all intersect; this point is a favored location for tornado development or redevelopment.

Tropopause The upper boundary of the troposphere, usually characterized by an abrupt change in the lapse rate from positive decreasing temperature with height, to neutral or negative, temperature constant or increasing with height.

Troposphere The layer of the atmosphere from the earth's surface up to the tropopause, characterized by decreasing temperature with height, vertical wind motion, appreciable water vapor content, and sensible weather (clouds, rain, etc.) See *Inverson, Cap.*

Trough An elongated area of relatively low atmospheric pressure, usually not associated with a closed circulation, and thus used to distinguish from a closed low. The opposite of ridge.

Turkey Tower [slang] A narrow, individual cloud tower that develops and falls apart rapidly. The sudden development of turkey towers from small cumulus clouds may signify the breaking of a cap.

Tonadic Vortex Signature TVS Doppler radar signature in the radial velocity field indicating intense, concentrated rotation, more so than a mesocyclone. Like the mesocyclone, specific criteria involving strength, vertical depth, and time continuity must be met in order for a signature to become a TVS. Existence of a TVS strongly increases the probability of a tornado occurrence, but does not guarantee it. A TVS is not a visually observable feature.

U

UKMETA medium-range weather predication model operated by the United Kingdom Meteorological Agency.

Unstable Air is unstable when moved either upward or downward, it continues to move in the same direction.

Updraft A small-scale current of rising air. If the air is sufficiently moist, then the moisture condenses to become a cumulus cloud or an individual tower of a towering cumulus or Cb.

Updraft Base-Alternative term for a rain-free base.

Upper Level System A general term for any large-scale or mesoscale disturbance capable of producing upward motion in the middle or upper parts of the atmosphere. This term is sometimes used interchangeably with *impulse* or *shortwave.*

Upslope Flow Air that flows toward higher terrain, and hence is forced to rise. The added lift often results in widespread low cloudiness and stratiform precipitation if the air is stable, or an increased chance of thunderstorm development if the air is unstable.

Upstream Toward the source of the flow, or located in the area from which the flow is coming.

Upward Vertical Motion or Velocity UVM or UVV.

V

Velocity Azimuth Display VAD A radar display on which mean radial velocity is plotted as a function or azimuth. See *VWP.*

Vault Same as Veering Winds Winds which shift in a clockwise direction with time at a given location such as from southerly to westerly, or which change direction in a clockwise sense with height such as southeasterly at the surface turning to southwesterly aloft. The latter example is a form of directional shear which is important for tornado formation. Compare with *Backing Winds.*

Vertically-Stacked System A low-pressure system, usually a closed low or cutoff low, which is not titled with height, i.e., located similarly at all levels of the atmosphere. Such systems typically are weakening and are slow-moving, and are less likely to produce severe weather than tilted systems. However, cold pools aloft associated with vertically-stacked systems may enhance instability enough to produce severe weather.

Vertically-Integrated Liquid water. A property computed by RADAP II and WSR-88D units that takes into account the three dimensional VIP-Video Integrator and Processor, which contours radar reflectivity (in dBZ) into six VIP levels. VIL

VIP 1 (Level 1, 18-30 dBZ) Light precipitation [square]

VIP 2 (Level 2, 30-38 dBZ) Light to moderate rain.

VIP 3 (Level 3, 38-44 dBZ0) Moderate to heavy rain

VIP 4 (Level 4, 44-50 dBZ) Heavy rain

VIP 5 (Level 5, 50-57 dBZ) Very heavy rain; hail possible

VIP 6 (Level 6, 57 dBZ) Very heavy rain and hail; large hail

Virga Steaks or wisps of precipitation falling from a cloud but evaporating before reaching the ground. In certain cases, shafts of Virga may precede a microburst; see *Dry Microburst.*

V Notch A radar reflectivity signature seen as a V-shaped notch in the downwind part of a thunderstorm echo. The V-notch is often seen on supercells, and is thought to be a sign of diverging flow around the main storm updraft and hence a very strong updraft. This term should not be confused with inflow notch or with enhanced V, although, the latter is believed to form by a similar process.

Volume Scan A radar scanning strategy in which sweeps are made at successive antenna elevations, i.e., a tilt sequence, and then combined to obtain the three-dimensional structure of the echoes. Volume scans are necessary to determine thunderstorm type and detect features such as WER's, BWER's, and overhang.

Vorticity A measure of the local rotation in a fluid flow. In weather analysis and forecasting, it usually refers to the vertical component of rotation, rotation about a vertical axis, and is used most often in reference to synoptic scale or mesoscale weather systems. By convention, positive values indicate cyclonic rotation.

Vort Max [slang] Short for vorticity maximum, a center, or maximum, in the vorticity field of a fluid.

VWP-VAD Wind Profile. A radar plot of horizontal winds, derived from VAD data, as a function of height above a Doppler Radar. The time-height display is plotted with height as the vertical axis and time as the horizontal axis, which then depicts the change in wind with time at various heights. This display is useful for observing local changes in vertical wind shear, such as backing of low-level winds, increases in speed shear, and development or evolution of nearby jet streams, including low-level jets.

W

Wall Cloud A localized, persistent, often abrupt lowering from a rain-free base. Wall clouds can range from a fraction of a mile up to nearly five miles in diameter, and normally are found on the south or southwest inflow, side of the thunderstorm. When seen from within several miles, many wall clouds exhibit rapid upward motion and cyclonic rotation; however, not all wall clouds rotate. Rotating wall clouds usually develop before strong or violent tornados, by anywhere from a few minutes up to nearly an hour. Wall clouds should be monitored visually for signs of persistent, sustained rotation and/or rapid vertical motion. "Wall Cloud" also is used occasionally in tropical meteorology to describe the inner cloud wall surrounding the eye of a tropical cyclone, but the proper term for this feature is eyewall.

Warm Advection Transport of warm air into an area by horizontal winds. Low-level warm advection is sometimes erroneously referred to as overrunning. Although the two terms are not properly interchangeable, both imply the presence of lifting in low levels.

Warning A product issued by NWS local offices indicating that a particular weather hazard is either imminent or has been reported. A warning indicates the need to take action to protect life and property. The type of hazard is reflected in the type of warning, e.g., tornado warning, blizzard warning. See *Short-Fuse Warning.*

Watch An NWS product indicating that a particular hazard is possible, i.e., that conditions are more favorable than usual for its occurrence. A watch is a recommendation to plan, to prepare, to be aware of changing weather to listen for further information, and to think about what to do if danger materializes.

Waterspout In general, a tornado occurring over water. Specifically, it refers to a small, relatively weak rotating column of air over water beneath a Cb or towering cumulus cloud. Waterspouts are most common over tropical or subtropical waters.

The exact definition of waterspout is debatable. In most cases the term is reserved for small vortices over water that are not associated with storm-scale rotation that is, they are the water-based equivalent of landspouts. But there is sufficient justification for calling virtually any rotating column of air a waterspout if it is in contact with a water surface.

Wedge or Wedge Tornado [slang] A large tornado with a condensation funnel that is at least as wide at the ground as it is tall from the ground to cloud base.

The term *wedge* is often is used somewhat loosely to describe any large tornado; however, not every large tornado is a wedge. A true wedge tornado, with a funnel at least as wide at the ground as it is tall, is very rare.

Wedges often appear with violent tornadoes, F4 or F5 on the Fujita Scale, but many documented wedges have been rated lower, and some violent tornadoes may not appear as wedges. For example, Xenia, OH on 3 April 1974 was rated F5 but appeared only as a series of suction vortices without a central condensation funnel. Whether or not a tornado achieves wedge status depends on several factors other than intensity—in particular, the height of the environmental cloud base and the availability of moisture below cloud base. Therefore, spotters should not estimate wind speeds or F-scale ratings based on visual appearance alone; however, it is generally safe to assume that most if not all wedges have the potential to produce strong, F2/F3, or violent, F4/F5, damage.

Weak Echo Region WER Radar term for a region of relatively weak overhang directly above it. The WER is a sign of a strong updraft on the inflow side of a storm, within which precipitation is held aloft. When the area of low reflectivity extends upward into, and is surrounded by, the higher relectivity aloft, it becomes a BWER.

Wet Microburst A microburst accompanied by heavy precipitation at the surface. A rain foot may be visible sign of a wet microburst.

Wind Shear See *Shear.*

Wrapping Gust Front A gust front which wraps around a mesocyclone, cutting off the inflow of warm moist air to the mesocyclone circulation and resulting in an occluded mesocylcone.

WSR-57, WSR-74 NWS Weather Surveillance Radar units, replaced by WSR-88D units.

WSR-88D Weather Surveillance Radar-1988 Doppler; NEXRAD unit.

Z

Zigzag Lightning Ordinary lightning of a cloud-to-cloud discharge that appears to have a single, but very irregular lightning channel. Viewed from the right angle, this may be observed as beaded lightning.

Zonal Flow Large-scale atmospheric flow in which the east-west component is dominant. The accompanying meridional component often is weaker than normal. Compare with *Meridional Flow.*